The Rev. Dr. Boyer bravely shares that which is kept secret by most. She teaches us what is possible to achieve, while suffering from what is normally a chronic, debilitating mental illness.

Carol Gonzales
R.N. and Certified End of Life Dula

Shalom is not an impossible dream for those struggling with a mental illness diagnosis. In sharing her personal story, written in the framework of Ecclesiastes 3:18, the Rev. Dr. Martha Boyer provides readers with hope for healing and wholeness of one's mind, body, and spirit from the mental anguish, loneliness, and isolation which often accompany such a diagnosis.

Especially insightful in this easy to read, self-help resource is the practical action steps and prayers included in each chapter. Thank you, Rev. Boyer for your honest disclosure of and your family's struggle with mental illness and for never giving up on the "impossible dream" of peace and well-being. This courageous book bears witness to the truth that there is "a time for everything in life and a time for every activity under heaven"—even seasons of mental anguish.

Rev. Laura C. Baker
Pastor, Starview United Church of Christ
Chaplain, Eagle Fire Co. #22
Mt. Wolf, PA

MY QUEST FOR SHALOM

Finding Peace in Mental Health

Martha Butkofsky Boyer

My Quest for Shalom

Finding Peace in Mental Health

Martha Butkofsky Boyer

Barber's Son Press
York, Pennsylvania

Published by

BARBER'S SON PRESS

York, Pennsylvania

© 2024 Martha Butkofsky Boyer. All rights reserved.

Edited by Pat Bonner and Christopher D. Rodkey.

Scripture quotations are from New Revised Standard Version of the Bible, copyright © 1989 National Council of the Churches of Christ in the United States of America. Used by permission. All rights reserved worldwide.

Other scripture quotations are taken from the KJV.

ISBN 978-1-7347188-6-7.

Library of Congress Control Number 9781734718867.

Front cover: In 1977, during her Christmas break from seminary studies in Costa Rica and Union Seminary (NYC), Martha shares her outer and inner wardrobe makeovers at home in Camp Hill, PA.

Back cover image: In 1977, Martha received practical theological training at this *barrio* called Chappulines built on a coffee plantation in San José, Costa Rica.

10 9 8 7 6 5 4 3 2 1

To all those who live with mental illness and their families, on their quests for Shalom.

TABLE OF CONTENTS

Acknowledgements   1

Introduction   3

Chapter 1   9
New Year's Eve, 1980, and New Year's Eve, 2022

Chapter 2   15
My Call to the Mission Field Accompanied by Farewells and Grief

Chapter 3   23
Istanbul and Conflicting Expectations

Chapter 4   27
The Great Disruption

Chapter 5   31
A Time To Be Born and a Time To Die

Chapter 6   41
A Time to Plant and a Time to Pluck Up What Has Been Planted

Chapter 7   49
A Time to Kill and a Time to Heal

Chapter 8   57
A Time to Break Down and a Time to Build

Chapter 9   69
A Time to Weep and a Time to Laugh

Chapter 10 75
A Time to Mourn and a Time to Dance

Chapter 11 83
A Time to Cast Away Stones,
and a Time to Gather Stones Together

Chapter 12 91
A Time to Embrace and a
Time to Refrain from Embracing

Chapter 13 99
A Time to Get and a Time to Lose

Chapter 14 107
A Time to Keep and a Time to Cast Away

Chapter 15 115
A Time to Rend and a Time to Sew

Chapter 16 123
A Time to Keep Silent and a Time to Speak

Chapter 17 131
A Time to Love and a Time to Hate

Chapter 18 139
A Time for War and a Time for Peace

Conclusion 147

A Prayer for Hope for Pastors
Facing Mental Health Challenges 150

Appendix 1 151
Resources

Appendix 2   153
*"A Theological-Educational
Experience in Latin America"*

Appendix 3   163
The Ministry Record of the Rev. Dr. Martha Boyer

Notes   165

ACKNOWLEDGEMENTS

To the congregations I have served throughout my 45 years of pastoral ministry, who provided their love and support throughout my quest for spiritual, mental, and physical well-being.

To all my fitness friends at the York Jewish Community Center for their joviality in the pool and gym.

To all my clergy colleagues in the York Association of the Penn Central Conference of the United Church of Christ for their collaborative efforts in ministry.

To the members of my family on earth who accompany me on "my quest for shalom," especially David, husband of 41 years; my son, Andrew; my sister, Karen Turner; cousins Mark and Connie Chen McConnell; my in-laws, Charlotte King, Sarah Webb and Richard and Lori Boyer.

To the members of my family in heaven who inspired and continue to inspire me on "my quest for shalom," especially my father, the Rev. Dr. Edward O. Butkofsky; my mother, the Rev. Mary Alice Butkofsky; my brother, Richard; my aunts, the Rev. Beatrice Weaver McConnell and Kathryn Moore; my uncle and music minister, Frank McConnell; and Grandpa and Grandma Howard and Daisy Weaver.

To Alyssa Boyer for use of communion photograph and The Church of the Brethren, *Messenger*, 2002 for permission to print photo of Mother in Washington Peace March.

To my friends, *compañeros*, and *Freunde* all around the world whose memories bring me so much joy!

To the Penn Central Conference Minister, Rev. Dr. Carrie Call, and Pastor Laura Baker for their prayerful presence throughout some of the deepest struggles of my life.

To all my neighbors at Powder Mill Apartments, who for the past twelve years have demonstrated to me how wonderful it is to live in a Shalom community!

To Pat Bonner, my editor, for her deep insights and gentle corrections.

INTRODUCTION

In the mid-1970s, I was among those twenty-year-olds who felt called to become a missionary. I began traveling to the most conflicted parts of the world with the desire to make a difference and promote peace. By 1980 I was living in Istanbul, Turkey, with ministerial standing and working for the United Church Board of World Ministries (UCBWM) of the United Church of Christ (UCC). A few days after Thanksgiving of that year, something happened that would change my life.

Strangely, I have no personal recollection of precisely what occurred other than my waking up in a French Hospital in Istanbul around Christmas. To my knowledge there are no medical records that provide insight into the incident or my treatment.

This time became a great secret.

For the next four decades I did not talk about this experience, as it evoked feelings of failure, shame, and bewilderment.

At the time, I just wanted to move on.

I did exactly what my doctors told me to do, and made every effort to recover as soon as possible from what I considered my "great fall." I tried to avoid the pitfall of Lot's wife, who turned into a pillar of salt when she looked back (Gen. 19:14). No one from the UCBWM asked me what happened. Former colleagues, pastors, and denominational representatives were also silent on my struggles, and I did not volunteer an explanation. Pastor Kendall Link from

Salem United Church of Christ (UCC) simply brought me a bouquet of flowers.

I suppressed any trace of memory deep in the recesses of my mind, unwilling to articulate the terror of what I had experienced or the hell in which I had been trapped. I embraced a personal goal to recover by settling into an apartment at Lancaster Theological Seminary used by missionaries on furlough.

Walking around on campus in Lancaster, Pennsylvania, I no longer heard speakers broadcasting prayers from minarets, nor did I hear the screeching of the *U-Bahn* tracks of West Berlin and subways in New York City. I did remember peering at the cloudy sky over the walls that surrounded West Berlin as well as the slow-paced strolls and lulling serenades with my *compañeros* in San José, Costa Rica. For in the three years that preceded my Istanbul experience, I had lived in four vastly different cultures, and had also backpacked through 17 other countries in Central America and Europe.

Suddenly thrust back into small-town life in Lancaster, I tried to adjust as quickly as possible to a new pattern of living. But I had no blueprint for my future. I was thinking I had failed as a pastor. I was feeling walled-in emotionally—more than I had felt physically confined by the walls of West Berlin that had surrounded my home for two years. I became determined to forget every traumatic detail of what happened to me in Istanbul. I vowed never to deal with what really happened until I would retire.

I retired on New Year's Eve, 2022, my last day Pastor of St. Paul United Church of Christ in Shrewsbury, Pennsylvania, and I was planning to fulfill my vow to deal with what happened to me in Istanbul. Family, friends, colleagues, and the congregation gathered to hear my farewell message, titled "The Final Word." I focused on the theme of my life's quest found in Ecclesiastes 3:1-8, namely, *Shalom*.

My words that night reflected upon my decades in ministry, but I also had a second speech in my heart that night that was never made. I did not mention my trauma in Istanbul because it would have required a longer explanation of what actually happened during that brief part of my ministry—even though that brief episode had significantly affected my entire ministry about which I had been speaking. Such an explanation might have diverted people from focusing on the more significant celebration of my 44 years of faithful ministry.

As I preached the message on New Year's Eve, I had a feeling of well-being; internally, I had already begun to deal with my trauma. During the Summer of 2021, I had started to look for a church to join in my retirement and to seek a pastor who I might be able to trust with my story.

What I did not share publicly on the day of my retirement is what I feel compelled to share here, now: the stark contrast between how I felt on New Year's Eve, 1980, and New Year's Eve, 2022. In this book, I will describe how my life evolved with the persistent challenges and triumphs that occurred throughout my life as a result of my ordeal in Istanbul.

Here I am exposing the details of my personal journey—and my clergy family's struggle—to understand mental illness as a pastor with a hope that my story will help other pastors who are trying to conceal a mental condition. My desire to help such persons is based on a belief that there is healing in disclosing mental anguish. I intend my story of healing will help relieve others of the loneliness and isolation that results from hiding a mental health challenge.

What I have learned can also help others build stronger relationships in every aspect of their lives.

Furthermore, this book is an attempt to show how I regained my sense of mission and my quest for Shalom—the wholeness of body, mind and spirit. To accomplish this, I use a framework based on Ecclesiastes 3:1-8 which relates that there is a time in life for everything and a time for every activity under heaven. The words are identified in the scripture as belonging to *Qoheleth* (the "Teacher"); the Talmud attributes the authorship of Ecclesiastes to King Solomon. Along with the phrases found in Ecclesiastes' 3:1-8, I have provided practical action steps, which I have discovered in my quest for Shalom.

I have been challenged by my family's experience with mental illness to earnestly seek this sense of peace. I have often doubted my own sanity and that of my family. I have wanted to make a contribution to society in spite of my fears that something within my immediate family and myself was not quite right. I longed for wellness and a sense of peace for myself and those around the world.

My longing is best described in the lyrics of Don Quixote de las Mancha's description of his quest, "To Dream the Impossible Dream." Don Quixote is thought to be insane in his quest for the "unreachable star." He is forced by his family and priest to come face to face with the "Knight of the Mirrors" in which he sees himself as he really is—a deranged old man. Then he sinks into deathly despair. In the end, he is revived by the song of Dulcinea, a whore. He calls her his lady who reminds him of his noble quest, to "reach" that "unreachable star," with a "heart stiving upward."[1]

I want to reach that unreachable star, striving for a sense of well-being not just for myself but for others. I believe that when such a universal state of "striving upward" is attained, we might together live in true and genuine Shalom communities.

Martha and her father hiking during her college years, 1975.

CHAPTER ONE

New Year's Eve, 1980,
and New Year's Eve, 2022

It was nearly dawn on New Year's Eve, 1980, in Istanbul, and I would soon to be on my way home to the United States. I was picked up from my apartment across the street from the Üsküdar American Academy complex. The school was one of five institutions operated by the Near East Mission Board which was an agency of the United Church Board for World Ministries (UCBWM) in Turkey. I had been employed in the Mission since early August of that year. Martha Millett, Principal of the Academy, rode next to me as my medical escort. She would accompany me from Istanbul through Frankfurt to John F. Kennedy (JFK) Airport in New York City. I was going back to the United States for a medical furlough of unknown duration.

It was also the Seventh Day of Christmas, but nostalgic refrains of "I'll Be Home for Christmas!" were not jingling around in my head. I was numb and my muscles were tight from the Haldol in my system. I was heavily drugged to block out some of the distress that I had experienced after Thanksgiving. My vision was blurred making it impossible for me to read or write.

I had been presented with a choice of where my new home in the States would be. A French doctor who had spoken to me when I first awoke in my hospital bed stated, "You have a choice of where to go: New York City, Lancaster, or Camp Hill." The UCBWM office was in New York; my mother lived in Camp Hill, Pennsylvania; I quickly answered,

"Lancaster—though I did not know just why I made that choice.

I was too heavily drugged to worry about where I was going or what was going to happen to me. I did, however, have an impending sense of doom that I was going home with my tail between my legs. I was ashamed to face or admit to anyone that I had failed as a missionary; I felt that my call to pastoral ministry, which began with my ordination at Salem UCC in Harrisburg, Pennsylvania (September 3, 1978), had been severed! The bewildering emotional upheaval that engulfed me had destroyed my hopes of finding a life partner, becoming a mother, and living a normal family life. At the age of 27, my professional and personal life had come to an end and my only hope was to go wherever I was directed and try to do everything that the mission board and the doctors advised me to do to survive.

Escorted by Martha Millett, I arrived safely to JFK airport, and was there met by the Penn Conference minister, Rev. Dr. Horace Sills and his wife Louise. A stranger named Melvin Wittler was also there. Melvin was to have been my boss in Istanbul, but he had been away on sabbatical the entire time that I had been there. As we exited the gate, he passed us on his way to board a plane to Istanbul where he would resume his work.

Horace told me that he was taking me to a furnished apartment that had been rented for me by the Board. Missionaries often spent their furloughs in residence at Lancaster Theological Seminary. It was a long drive to Lancaster from JFK. I gazed out the car windows trying to focus on familiar billboards that would help me accept the fact that I was back in the United States, not still surrounded by bazaars, bakeries with fresh loaves of bread and Baklava, butcher shops displaying large hanging carcasses of raw meat, Oriental rug shops and apartments built on the hillsides above the Bosporus—all prominent features of my Istanbul neighborhood. During the nearly four-hour trip, Horace spoke of his concern for my brother Richard who was being treated for chronic schizophrenic episodes that had plagued him since his beating as a youth during junior high school racial riots.

Horace sharply disagreed with my mother on the proper treatment for Richard. He asserted my brother should be admitted into the state psychiatric hospital in Harrisburg. Horrified by the conversation, I silently continued the drive. If I mentioned what I had experienced in Istanbul, I feared Horace might drive me directly to the same hospital and admit me! I experienced such relief when we exited the highway near Lancaster, that we did not continue on to Harrisburg.

Instead, we entered the driveway of Lancaster Theological Seminary. Louise and Horace led me into an apartment in Harner Hall that had been furnished for my use during my medical furlough. They departed and I was left alone on New Year's Eve, 1980. Louise promised to return a few days later to take me to a beautician and take me to psychiatrist for an evaluation.

The new year was going to be a time for an extreme adjustment on my part. Besides the new cultural setting, there was nothing on my calendar but an appointment with a psychiatrist in a few days. With very few memories of what had happened in my life since Thanksgiving, I sat in that apartment alone, pondering a future that would most likely exclude a partner, offspring, and lucidity. I strained to think of something for which to be grateful, and I found it: I was home and safe in the United States—far away from the perilous streets of Istanbul. I began to feel a sense of relief. No matter what horror I had just experienced, I now had a safe refuge at the seminary where I might begin to figure out what had happened to me during my last months in Istanbul.

Exactly forty-two years later, on New Year's Eve, 2022, at the age of 69 I was now facing another life transition. Though there were some elements of the day that were similar, the circumstances were much more positive. I was once again in the presence of the Conference Minister, but it was not Rev. Dr. Horace Sills and his wife. This time it was Rev. Dr. Carrie Call and her husband, Dr. Randall Zachman. Carrie had come to participate in the farewell liturgy at St. Paul United Church of Christ in Shrewsbury, Pennsylvania. Prior to the service, Carrie and Randall joined my family for a dinner celebration at my home near York. That day, I also had the support of my new pastor, Rev. Laura Baker of Starview United Church of Christ in York, where my family planned to transfer the next day.

I remembered the dismal doom of those forty-two years prior, when I had felt destined to a life without a partner and offspring. But I was now rejoicing with my husband of almost 40 years, David, and our son, Andrew, 35. I was on my way to celebrate not the funeral of a career, but rather 44 years of ministry in which I had served eight churches in addition to my work in Costa Rica, West Germany, and Turkey.

Though I did not mention these contrasts in my final message, I was inwardly singing the sentiments of so many hymn writers who had experienced similar dramatic contrasts in their lives with trauma and spiritual resurrection: "*Amazing grace*, how sweet the sound that saved a wretch like me; I once was lost but now I'm found!" "When sorrows like sea billows roll, whatever my lot, Thou has taught me to say, 'It is well, *it is well with my soul!*'"

Forty-two years had passed. between those two New Year's Eves. One began with fear and bewilderment; the other began with joyful anticipation. Both ended with feelings of deep gratitude. I asked myself on December 31, 2022, "Why did I wait so long to deal with what happened to me in Istanbul?" This insight made me wonder: *What would have happened if I dealt with the trauma earlier, and more openly?*

It is now my thesis that if I had dealt with what happened years earlier, I would have received more help and found healing much sooner. So I write this story, painful though it is to live through and revisit the memories, with the hope that you, reader, might learn from my mistakes. I pray that you might be more open and willing to deal with mental injury as it occurs in your life and not postpone facing it, like me, at a future retirement.

As a teenager in the 1960s, Martha Helene Butkofsky developed a fascination with the cultural heritage of New York City, which fueled her desire to explore the world in her own community.

CHAPTER TWO

My Call to the Mission Field
Accompanied by Farewells and Grief

What was so horrible, that I kept it hidden for forty years and suppressed it until 2021? For me to understand my ordeal in Turkey, I had to first revisit the period of time that preceded my journey there. I believe it probably started on the pier of a harbor in Salem, Massachusetts, during a United Church Board of World Missions (UCBWM) meeting in 1976 when I first felt a "call" to serve as a new kind of mission partner. This particular harbor was where the very first Congregational missionaries had left, years before, on their way to Hawaii. Coincidentally, "Salem" also means "Shalom,"

My First Significant Farewell

Acknowledging my call, I requested and received a grant from the UCBWM for one year of study at the Seminario Bíblico Latineramericano (SBL) in San José, Costa Rica. Within a few months, I was departing the Harrisburg, Pennsylvania, Greyhound Station on an eleven-stop journey to San José where I studied with students from nineteen different Latin American countries. This one year at the Seminario was an emotional period, as I established deep friendships and experienced intense theological study with the other students and faculty. We debated the issues of peace, for they felt passionate about the highly volatile politics of their countries. We found hope in revelations of Biblical hope. Our class' essays were published into a Spanish book on Revelation.

I also developed intense relationships with the members of a coffee plantation church in Chappulines, San José. With nowhere else to go, people working on the plantation constructed shacks using building materials from abandoned homes. When they heard of a house that had been abandoned, they simply took the materials in the middle of the night to build additions onto their own one room homes. I spent two nights in one of these shacks along with a family of two parents and five children, along with three dogs, two cats, six chickens and twelve hatching eggs. The only water was from a faucet in the mud streets. There were TV antennas on most tin roofs. The TVs inside the huts were connected to large batteries.

The plantation's one-room church was constructed of wood. While sitting on the few simple logs or standing in the vast gathering area, the adults and children worshiped and sang joyously. They often sang *"Alabaré a mi Señor"* ("Praise to the Lord"), accompanied by guitars and an accordion.

One night, I decided to stay in the village. I preached in Spanish to a chapel overflowing with worshipers of all ages. Perhaps the chapel was so full because they wanted to hear what I had to say after having lived in one of their huts. I don't remember what I preached that night, but I seem to remember it had something to do with the incarnation of Christ. God came down to earth to be right there with them, just as one of them.

I earnestly wanted to understand their way of life. I remember that in class, the next day after my overnight adventure, the SBL professor taught that Jesus did indeed come down to earth as the Savior to live like one of us. But because of the incarnation, we do not need to go and move in with the poor. I still wonder, however, how radically we must change our lifestyle when we choose to live among the poor? Mother Teresa of Calcutta lived heroically among the poor. I wondered: *What kind of lifestyle change was I being challenged to make by the new consciousness developing within me?* Many of my fellow students struggled financially, and some had walked from homes in South America to Costa Rica in order to study at the SBL!

There are so many other stories I could share—including the time I almost drowned in the Pacific Ocean. My friend Javier Torres from Venezuela could not swim but his heroic efforts encouraged me to keep fighting the undertow. I was asking God "Is this the end?" when the current shifted and I was able to slowly drift to safety. Much relieved, we three *compañeros* sang joyously with guitars on the train ride back from our remote beach trip.

My first significant farewell from the mission field was just after Thanksgiving in 1977 when I left San José. At the SBL, it was tradition to serenade those celebrating a special occasion. I was present at every serenade playing my flute, while student Isaias Pecho from Peru played his guitar. On the eve of my departure, the group surprised me with a serenade. I joined my *compañeros* singing and playing my flute. Today I cherish a cassette recording of this final serenade.

The next morning, I departed San José with Linda Garcia and Jerjes Ruiz. The three of us began our trip by bus up the Pan-American Highway towards Florida, stopping at every Christmas Marketplace in every major capital city of Central America from Costa Rica to Mexico City. A poet and new seminary graduate, Jerjes would later become the President of the Baptist Seminary in war-torn Managua, Nicaragua.

I left Latin America having gained a myriad of experiences including the very intense farewell. I was looking forward to my next adventure. But I still needed to return to Union Theological Seminary in New York City to complete my final semester of study and my master's thesis. In addition, I needed to write a report summarizing my Costa Rican experience. A month later, that report would be published in an international missiological journal.*

In May, 1978, I graduated from Union Theological Seminary and was ordained on September 3 of the same year at my home church, Salem UCC in Harrisburg, Pennsylvania. On the day I was ordained, I had appeared with my father—also a pastor—on the front page of the *Harrisburg Patriot-News* under the headline "Ministry Doings All in the Family." My father was well-known as a life-long pastor in the United Church of Christ: he had been active on several college boards of trustees; chaired the Latin American Committee of The UCBWM; served as President of the Board of Bethany Children's Home; served on the Hymnal Committee of the Evangelical and Reformed Church; and as part of the National Synod movements in Cleveland to form the UCC in 1957. One week after my ordination, I was on a plane for my first call to parish ministry in West Berlin.

More Farewells and Grief

Once in Germany, my work evolved primarily around youth education. I assisted in teaching four weekly confirmation classes with about 15 students each. In the evenings I helped the parish social worker with the *Jugend Kellar*—the "Youth Cellar" in the basement of the church. There young people gathered for nightly conversation in a coffee-house

---

* This article is found in Appendix Two of this book, beginning on page 153.

setting. I also accompanied the confirmation students on numerous overnight retreats through West Germany. My other church duties included meeting with church staff, planning sessions with the pastor, and serving as Christian educator for special worship services.

My work in West Germany was challenging and, at times, disturbing. I toured several concentration camps while living and working for 10 days with the Dietrich Bonhoeffer Church Youth in the former SS Barracks of Auschwitz. We toured the gas showers and the ovens. We viewed display cases of flesh tattoos and storerooms of prosthetics. It was not until seven months later in Istanbul that the trauma of that experience surfaced, as I had the delusion I was being chased in Auschwitz by the SS police.

In June, 1980, I received a job offer by mail in West Berlin, Germany. It was from Elinor Galusha, Director of Personnel for the UCBWM in New York City. Elinor asked me to consider coming home to the US in mid-July to pack for a new more permanent appointment in Turkey. Since I had almost completed my second year as a Fraternal Worker and Associate Missionary in West Germany, and had been asked to extend my term for a third year, I had a decision to make.

A couple months earlier, I had initiated a discussion of what opportunities were available in Latin America or Israel. I longed to return for service in Latin America. At the SBL in Costa Rica, I had completed one of the three years needed to receive my Master of Divinity Studies from Union Theological Seminary in NYC. But the hostage crises of the 1970's and the violence in the Middle East continued to dominate the news and I was also intrigued by the thought of serving there,

One month after receiving the new job offer from UCBWM, I resigned my position at the Dietrich Bonhoeffer Church and returned home to Camp Hill, Pennsylvania, for a two-week break. I would be packing for a five-year appointment as Executive Assistant at the Near East Mission in Istanbul, Turkey.

My farewell from the Dietrich Bonhoeffer Church in West Berlin had been deeply moving. Members of the parish church crossed the wall to East Berlin to have a picnic lunch in the fields of a park in a remote location. We had a simple picnic feast, sharing family stories and enjoying a "thanksgiving" picnic together.

Right before I waved good-bye, all the church members from the East and West gathered. They formed a large circle, and each person gave me a hug. Walking away in the distance, I could still hear them singing and motioning *"Er hält die Ganze Welt in seiner Hand"* ("He Has the Whole World in His Hands"). I left this scene directly for the airport in West Berlin, where two of my favorite youth group members gave me a final goodbye hug at the gate. As I said farewell, I experienced a sense of anticipation and adventure of what might lie ahead.

The next day, I was in New York City being interviewed for employment in Istanbul, Turkey. I was briefed for my mission by Board personnel Dale Bishop and Rev. Elinor Galusha. After being cleared medically and spending a night in a hotel, I took the train to the station in Harrisburg, Pennsylvania, which is just across the Susquehanna River from my hometown of Camp Hill. I was welcomed home by my mother, sister Karen and brother Richard. My father resided about 80 miles away in Phoebe Nursing Home in Allentown, Pennsylvania.

During the two weeks that I was "home" in the United States, I attended a national United Church of Christ Christian educator conference with my mother in New Hampshire; hosted Hajo Curth, a pastor from West Berlin, and his family on their trip to Wilmington, Delaware; and was commissioned as a missionary in my home church—Salem UCC, Harrisburg. The Central Association of the Penn Central Conference of the UCC also honored me by appointing me their "adopted missionary" and sponsored an association event and radio interview.

While with my mother visiting in New England for a UCC conference, we received a call from Rev. Dr. Horace Sills that my father had suddenly become critically ill and had been taken to St. Luke's Hospital with pneumonia. We quickly returned home. When I entered his room, he was wearing an oxygen mask. I don't recall what I said, but I am sure I told him that I loved him and how much he meant to me. All that I can remember of that moment with my father were his final and only words: "It was all very beautiful."

Two Celebration of Life Services were held for my father less than a week later. I will always be grateful to the Dietrich Bonhoeffer church for having gifted me with a trip home to the US for a two-week Christmas vacation home in 1979 so that I could visit my father before his unexpected passing the following summer. I received flowers from the UCBWM.

My brother Richard experienced a major psychotic episode at our father's funeral. I still see him rolling on the carpet of the office entrance, deeply disturbed and grieving. A day later, I took him to see one of the *Star Wars* episodes during which he described seeing *Star Wars*' character faces on the people surrounding him.

As for my mission in Istanbul, I never considered postponing my trip. An orientation for language studies and teaching for the newest class of educators at the mission school was about to begin. I had packing to do. I know now that I rushed through my grief process.

Richard was my close buddy. As I prepared for Turkey, he helped me pack for Turkey. We enjoyed drinking his homemade dandelion wine together. On one occasion, we drank his wine and smoked cigars in father's basement office. The next day, my mother drove my brother and me to Stone Harbor, New Jersey, to jump the waves of the Atlantic Ocean and to sleep for one night at the Pebbles Guest House.

The following day, Mother drove me to Philadelphia to board the plane for Istanbul. Within two turbulent weeks, I had said goodbye to my friends in Germany; participated in mission deprogramming and orientation; fulfilled speaking engagements, said a final farewell to my father; packed what I would need for my new mission; and, once again, left the remainder of my family and home in the United States. As I said farewell to all of these, I was whisked off to Istanbul where I said *"Merhaba"* to Istanbul, Turkey.

CHAPTER THREE

Istanbul and Conflicting Expectations

I arrived at the Near East Mission Office in Istanbul, Turkey, in August of 1980. The Mission Office oversaw a hospital; administration of three private American English-speaking schools; and the Red House Printing Press, which was famous for its Turkish-English dictionaries. With a five-year contract, my new role would be as Executive Assistant for the Near East Mission—replacing the previous assistant, Frances Eddy, who had just retired after more than 40 years' service.

During my orientation, I was warned that there was a tense situation in the office where I was to be employed. The Mission Secretary and Director, who had recruited me as a Mission Partner, was on sabbatical and would remain so until January 1, 1981. The situation was described as transitional, stressed ,and in need of a pastoral figure to help support relationships among the mission personnel. A primary goal was to give the Turkish national staff positions greater responsibility within both the Mission Office and the mission field itself.

This warning further complicated my understanding of what my role would be. During my orientation in New York City, I had been cautioned not to assume the same role as the long-tenured assistant, Frances Eddy. My role would be quite different so that Turkish nationals working at the Mission Office would take a greater lead. This change supported the desire of the UCBWM to transfer more responsibility to national mission partners around the world, which was the approach I had studied while at the seminary in Costa Rica.

UCBWM staff outlined three priorities for my mission work. First, I was to learn the Turkish language as soon as possible, which meant intensive language study together with two other persons recently employed as the new editors of the Red House Press. Second, I was to be a pastoral figure to the mission personnel who were experiencing power struggles in the office due to exit of the long-tenured Executive Assistant (Eddy) and the sabbatical absence of an Executive (Wittler). Finally, I was charged to write missionary letters to stateside churches, including churches the Central Association of the Penn Central Conference which had a special relationship with me.

Upon my arrival in Turkey, I discovered that the expectations of my local, "acting boss" in the office were very different, if not contradictory. In the sabbatical absence of the Executive, the Vice Executive had taken charge of the Mission Office. The dynamic was complicated by the fact that the Vice Executive's wife was my mentor.

Despite the conflicting views, I decided to productively move forward to the extent it was possible. One thing that was not in dispute was my need to learn Turkish. I focused on learning the language with the hope I would be fluent by the time the Office Executive returned the in the following January from his sabbatical. I also attempted to develop pastoral type relationships with the individuals working in the Mission Office, who included about ten Turkish nationals, the Vice Executive, myself, and one other person. To my dismay, I immediately discovered that only three of the Turkish nationals spoke English. The Office Manager, who had been identified to take my role as the Executive Assistant when I would eventually depart, spoke very little English.

I was experiencing the dysfunction and tension in the office of which I had been warned. In the office, I chose not to disagree with the Executive Vice President and his wife when there was a conflict between the expectations established in New York and what I was being told to do by those in Istanbul. Instead, I complied when possible or responded with silence and withdrawal. My last missionary letter to stateside churches was about the military coup on September 12, 1980. After this, I felt I had reached a point where I was unable to write anything positive.

When the Vice Executive told me of an upcoming visit to Istanbul by the Middle Eastern Secretary of the UCBWM along with Avery Post, President the United Church of Christ, and Kenneth Teegarden, President of the Disciples of Christ (Christian Church), I decided to write a letter. On my 27th Birthday—Halloween, 1980—I typed a letter to the two UCBWM administrators in New York who had initially briefed me on my role at the office. I explained that there was a discrepancy in expectations between my "acting boss" in Istanbul and what they had told me before I had left. I requested a meeting to resolve the inconsistencies.

The visit with mission personnel was to be Thanksgiving Day at the Üsküdar American Academy. Knowing mail would take at least 11 days to arrive in NYC, I wrote my concerns directly to the Middle East Secretary and the Personnel Director with the hope that they might respond to my concern before or when the delegation arrived in Turkey. This letter was mailed about November 1, 1980—a day after my birthday.

I awaited a response. In the meantime, I was asked to visit the American School in Tarsus to speak with its Principal, who was also the Chairman of the Near East Mission Board. I sought some spiritual refreshment on the 9-hour trip to Tarsus in a sleeping car with a Turkish family of seven people who spoke only Turkish. I wrote home about this experience. I told how the strangers in the train so generously shared their Turkish Delight and baked goods as I shared my raw figs. I was so pleased to finally be able to communicate solely in Turkish. There was also my excitement to be able to visit Paul's hometown (Tarsus) and the well from which he had drawn water. It was a truly beautiful and restful trip.

I returned to Istanbul and continued my Turkish language study and office work, still waiting for an answer to my letter and the impending arrival of the denominational executives on Thanksgiving Day. When they arrived, I gave President Post and his wife a tour of the Blue Mosque. The next day, we all shared Thanksgiving Dinner at the Üsküdar School.

Given that I had not yet received a response to my letter, I had expected a response during the visit. But no one mentioned it as we celebrated. No one asked me how I was doing. I did not discuss my concerns to the Secretary of the Mission who appeared busy entertaining the top executives of the churches and the Vice Executive. As the day progressed, I withdrew deeper into my shell of discomfort. The visitors left on the Monday immediately following Thanksgiving.

CHAPTER FOUR

The Great Disruption

With Thanksgiving and the visit over, I resumed my Turkish lessons. I found my ability to converse during my next lesson particularly difficult as I had trouble concentrating. At the end of class, I left my tutor and fellow students. Feeling too ill to go to work, I took a taxi, the ferry, and another taxi back to my apartment.

A heavy blanket of stress enveloped me, and I repeated Psalm 23 in a fervent prayer to make it home safely. As I approached my apartment, I felt more stressed than I had ever experienced before. Recognizing that I had no phone or other means of communication in my apartment should I become further debilitated, I decided to cross the street towards the Üsküdar School and the apartment of the school's Principal, Martha Millett. I wasn't certain that I would be able to make it without falling over in the street where I feared no one would help me, but I continued to recite the 23rd Psalm to myself with the hope that I would find refuge with Martha and that she could let the Near East Mission Office know that I was too sick to come to work.

I was so relieved when Martha Millett answered the door and welcomed me into her home. Within moments, I fell to the floor and slid across it on my stomach before assuming a catatonic position peering out the patio doors at the walls which surrounded the Üsküdar School complex. At this point, I entered a terrifying state of delusion in which I believed I was being pursued by the Nazis and incarcerated at Auschwitz.

My illness caused many blackout periods and as a result, I do not recall how I came to be admitted to the French Hospital. I do know that a day or so after I awakened, I requested hospital personnel release me for a day so I could visit the church I had been attending during my residence in the city–the Union Church of Istanbul. The sanctuary was filled with poinsettias, so it must have been almost Christmas.

I may never have any recollection of what happened to me during those blackout periods. I only remember brief conversations with a bilingual psychiatrist who told me, "You have to go home on a medical furlough. The Mission Board discussed sending you to Ankara for treatment but decided that you would get better rehabilitation in the United States. So, they are sending you home on a medical furlough. Another reason for sending you to the US is that your brother, Richard, has been very ill since your father's funeral. The Conference Minister, Horace Sills, and your mother are fighting about what is best for him. Dr. Sills believes that Richard should be placed in the State Hospital in Harrisburg. You must go home. Where do you want to live? NYC, Lancaster, or Camp Hill?" I simply answered. "Lancaster."

During the days following Christmas, I was heavily drugged, but I was recovered enough to stay in my Istanbul apartment and pack my personal belongings for the trip back to the US. I was not yet able to comprehend what had happened to me after Thanksgiving, but I did know I had made a conscious decision to try to forget whatever had happened. I chose to suppress it and get on with my life as quickly as possible. I would attempt to put off dealing with the trauma until I retired!

Though I carried the weight of what had happened to me during the next 42 years, I did not receive an accurate diagnosis for my condition until August 31, 2022! Such a diagnosis was only made possible because I was planning my upcoming retirement. I started to open up about what had happened to me.

First, I met with Rev. Laura Baker, the Pastor of Starview United Church of Christ (York, Pennsylvania) in the Summer of 2021. Then I began talking with the Conference Minister, Rev. Carolyne Call, in May, 2022. I enrolled in "Spiritual and Personal Development," a course Dr. Call was teaching as part of the Pennsylvania Academy of Religion at Lancaster Theological Seminary. As a final assignment for that course, students were challenged to write a case study about a ministry that, according to the syllabus, "contained some of the following: high anxiety, emotional cutoff, emotional reactivity, triangles, fusion or other aspects from the readings." We were to write a case study on an "event that did not end well or left you in a bad place emotionally."

For the assignment, I chose to write a case study of what happened to me in Istanbul in 1980. The task helped me not only analyze what had gone wrong. It also helped restore many of my memories regarding my work at the Near East Mission. When I left Turkey so suddenly, I had no time to say good-bye. My grieving process was cut short. Despite its sudden end, I had many good experiences in Istanbul: socializing with the other mission partners, living in an apartment, enjoying the Baklava and fresh bread that I smelled each morning baking below my apartment, eating fresh fish caught on the Bosporus, touring the bazaars, hiking and visiting many Biblical sites. As memorable as these experiences were, they were blotted from my memory for a long time due to my trauma and abrupt return from Istanbul.

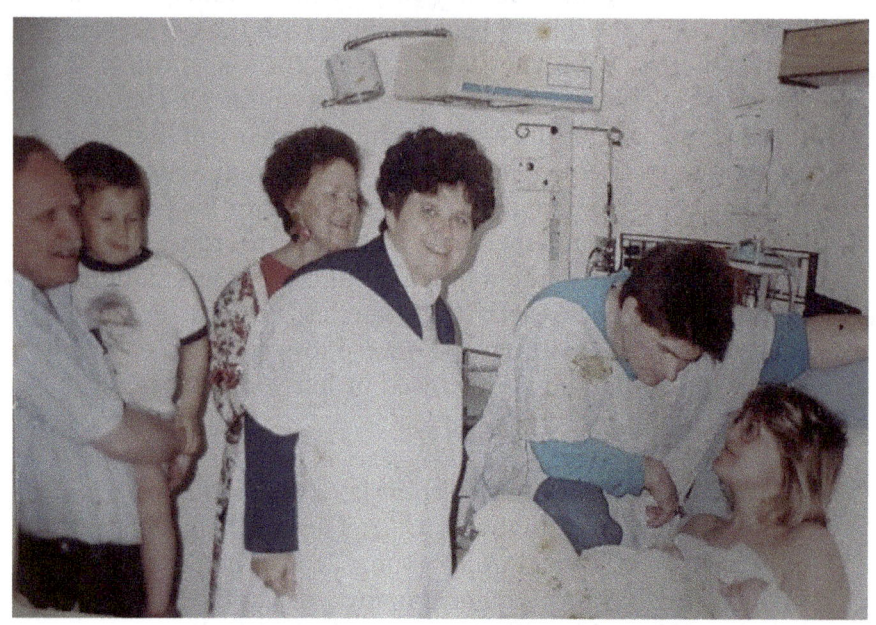

Baby Elizabeth (niece) with David, Andrew, Mother, Martha, Nelson, and Karen (sister).

CHAPTER FIVE

A Time To Be Born and a Time To Die

(Ecclesiastes 3:2)

A Time to Be Born

It was my time to be born and the obstetrician went hunting. My life began with a sense of urgency which has characterized my entire life. It was Halloween Day/Reformation Day, October 31, 1953. When my mother (Mary Alice Weaver Butkofsky) called the obstetrician to tell him she was experiencing labor pains, he simply responded "No baby today. I'm going hunting." When it became apparent that I would not wait, my father—Rev. Dr. Edward O. Butkofsky—drove through five red lights to get my mother to St. Luke's Hospital in Bethlehem, Pennsylvania. Just as my mother was being wheeled out of the elevator, I was born.

Although I was received with joy, I was not the hoped-for baby boy that they had expected would be a future minister. My older sister, Karen, born two years prior, had also similarly not been the hoped-for gender that my parents had written about in a note dated 1951. I found the note a few years ago in which they related their great anticipation of a son who would become a minister. Slides of my early childhood show me well-groomed in tailored attire and a pixie haircut, in contrast to the colorful, frilly attire and long hair that I would prefer in later years.

The certain urgency and anxiety surrounding my birth was also related to having lost her first child—a son. My brother, John Howard Butkofsky, died on the first day of his life, March 15, 1950. Mother often repeated the story of Johnny whose death was blamed on her over-medication to delay his birth till it was more convenient for the doctor. The drugs made it too difficult for little John to expel mucus after his birth. Mother's grief over the loss of her first son colored all three of her later birthing experiences.

The tragic death even shaped her reaction more than three decades later when my own son Andrew was born on December 18, 1987. Mother did not announce Andrew's birth to any of her friends for days after she became a grandma for fear her first grandson, born nine weeks prematurely, would die just as her first son and my husband David's older brother, Homer Boyer, Jr. had also tragically died.

The sense of urgency at my birth, sometimes appearing to others as an unhealthy impatience, has become a character trait. Compounding this impatience to embrace every moment of my life is the fear that I might also experience the fate of my father. As I write this book, I am just five years younger than when my father—at age 74—began showing signs of dementia that forced his retirement as a pastor. His dementia increased so that on the weekend of my graduation from Union Seminary in New York City, he was found wandering around Riverside Drive in his pajamas. He had had plans to write a book that he never completed so now I feel even more resolve to complete mine.

ACTION STEP #1

Take Time to Reflect

When we live life with a sense of urgency and impatience, we often forfeit living within the natural rhythm of our environment. We fail to be sensitive to people and nature around us.

As we speed down the freeway at 70 miles per hour or rush through the stores to get home in time for microwave meals, we risk breakdowns similar to overworked machinery on an assembly line. Our bodies are not machines.

When we get caught up in the speed cycles of life, we forget why we are doing what we are doing as Martha did in the Biblical Story of Martha and Mary. In contrast, Mary took time to listen to Jesus and reflect.

The urgency we may feel has an antidote and that is prayer and reflection. Reflection is the first stop on my quest for shalom.

Decades of counseling with a variety of therapists (psychologists, psychiatrists, social workers and pastors) and academic reflection has given me many opportunities to reflect upon the challenges of my mental health episodes and symptoms. Knowing one's triggers, as well as early symptoms are critical to remaining stable. Having tools for self-reflection help provide a systematic framework for assessing one's life, family and social interactions, and mission.

The phrase, "know thyself," dates to Socrates. Aristotle also said, "Knowing yourself is the beginning of all wisdom." This is good advice for all in our present age, not only those with mental health challenges but for life, in general.

Prayer

O God, Forgive my urgent pace.

Slow me down so that I might take the proper time to navel-contemplate, to discover from whence I came, who I am now, and where I am going.

Help me to find the right person with whom to reflect upon my life, so that I may truly know myself in a manner that helps me to grow.

Then, please give me bold courage to take a good look at myself in the mirror and to see myself as you see me, a beloved Child of God.

Amen.

A Time to Die

I remember the moment when I first expressed my fear of death. I was five as I hurried down the stairs of Salem UCC's parsonage to where my mother was rocking in a chair. I jumped into her arms and blurted out the words, "I don't want to die!" Why do people have to die?"

Although I did not tie all the events together at the time, I realize in retrospect that this was the same year that my maternal grandmother, Daisy Weaver, died at the age of 78. I remember her funeral service at the funeral home next to Christ Church UCC in Bethlehem, Pennsylvania. I touched Grandma's stone-cold cheek and felt the lifeless shell of the warm body that had frequently shared a room with me at her home in Bethlehem. The fresh smell of spring flowers is a fragrance I recall each Easter and with every Celebration of Life observance.

At Butkofsky family plots, Oddfellow's Cemetery, Shamokin, PA, August, 2023.

It was an incomprehensible loss. Grandma was the one who cut rhubarb from her garden to make tart pies. A great cook, she served the best family chicken dinners with buttered mashed potatoes and peas. She placed black licorice jellybeans and ribbon candy on the buffet to entice her grandchildren. It was this grandmother who had delighted with Cootie, Parcheesi, and the Ouija Board. Sister Karen and I had often fought to share a room with Grandma, making fun of her false teeth in the cup of water on the nightstand. Now, she would no longer be there for us in the granite cottage under the Big Star in the mountains of Bethlehem for Christmas visits. I no longer had what all of my first-grade friends seemed to have, a grandma.

As a widower, Grandpa Howard (Weaver) lived another six years. I slowly watched him decline and age after Grandma's death. He stayed for the most part in their Bethlehem home attended by a caregiver, but in the mid-1960s he had to move to the Muhlenberg Hospital where he lived his final years before passing in 1965.

His actual death was not as traumatic for me as my grandma's, but what followed affected me quite profoundly. Grandpa owned a farm with considerable acreage and several rental properties before he retired. When the will was read by the lawyers, a battle over the immense estate ensued. This was a battle between my mother on one side and my Aunts Bea and Kaye on the other side. Aunt Bea is known within UCC circles as the Rev. Beatrice Weaver McConnell, the first woman graduate of Lancaster Theological Seminary. She began studies at Lancaster Theological seminary on *November 8, 1945*, at the age of. 22. On June 13, 1948, she then became the first woman ordained in the Evangelical and Reformed Church. As the youngest daughter of my grandpa, Aunt Bea was named Executrix in his will. My mother complained that Aunt Bea had stolen the birthright from her (the middle sister) when their older sister Kay declined to oversee the estate.

At the time of Grandpa's death, I was 11 and this clash left me deeply conflicted. How could seminary graduates, who preached about loving God and neighbor and who served as ordained clergy, be drawn into such an estate battle? When my grandfather died, I had felt a strong call to the ministry just as I had at age five when Grandma had died. However, I said "no" because of the intensity of the legal battle among my family members over the estate.

The dispute calmed down in 1973 when I hosted a surprise party at Salem UCC for my parents' 25th wedding anniversary. I invited the entire wedding party which included my Aunt Bea. But the old quarrel resurfaced when Grandpa's brother and my Great Uncle, Stewart Howard, died in 1977—Aunt Bea was again named Executrix. According to my Cousin Mark, who was Bea's son, the hard feelings resulting from the estate dispute were why my Aunt Bea attended neither my mother's ordination in 1977 nor my ordination in 1978. At the time, I was unaware of the reason that she had declined my personal invitation to participate in my ordination service.

Dr. Mark McConnell, my cousin, and I have long observed and discussed the lifelong dispute between our mothers that kept them apart for over forty years. Cousin Mark and I agree that Aunt Bea was asked by her father to oversee his estate because he recognized the organizational ability of his youngest daughter and trusted her to manage the estate. There was no overt favoritism. Without discrediting my mother's other abilities, we all knew my mother simply did not have the knowledge and skills required to manage the financial complexities of an estate.

I began to dream of peace and reconciliation. While I could intuitively take sides with my aunt, I did not express my opinion to my family. I simply continued to feel sickened by the dispute. Mark, who was five years younger, says he did not realize the impact the family fight had on my life. He was initially shielded from the funeral and inheritance debates; it was not until later that he became aware of the conflict.

Cousin Mark and I spoke often of trying to reconcile our mothers, though we could not predict how they might treat one another if they met face to face. In the summer of 2016—a full half century since the passing of my Grandpa Howard and the birth of the quarrel, Mark called me to say the time had come to try. I picked up Mother at the Brethren Home where she resided, and we drove to Willow Valley where Aunt Bea lived. When we entered the television lounge where Aunt Bea was sitting in her power chair listening to Hillary Clinton's campaign speech, they immediately found a common accord regarding politics and the national election. The visit was a short but amiable first step.

I don't believe that they fully reconciled until a year later. Mark encouraged me to arrange one final meeting between our mothers. This time, Mother was quite anxious to see her sister. Their behavior displayed discomfort and dissonance but enough compassion to satisfy me that they had truly reconciled. After the meeting, I immediately phoned Mark to tell him of my joy that the two seemed at peace with one another. Aunt Bea passed not long after in 2018, and Mother followed in 2019.

ACTION STEP #2

Take Time to Build Support Systems

I began my "quest for shalom" early in my life, while surrounded by what seemed to me to be endless family estate and church conflicts. Experiencing church conflict of a young age is not uncommon for "PKs," that is, a Preacher's Kid. But I was a "PKPKPN"—Preacher's Kid-Preacher's Kid-Preacher's Niece, doubly a preacher's kid and preacher's niece. All of that being said, from an early age, I believed life did not have to be like that in my family or in church life. I knew that this family conflict is just not the way that God intends family life to be. Conflicts should and can be resolved as beautifully as how the dominant chords of Mozart reach beautiful harmonic resolutions.

When we live with family tension or church conflict that disrupts our sense of wellness, it is important to partner with other family and members to try to reconcile the battling parties. It may take years to heal wounds because of an irrational buildup of emotions and breakdowns in trust. In my family, it took fifty years. The prospective length of recovery is not a reason to give up on trying to reconcile parties.

The surprise party that I had hosted in 1973 alleviated some of the heartache and served to partially reconcile my mother and aunt, but the wound still festered for a long time after that. Hours and hours of phone calls between Cousin Mark and me and other family discussions helped us to deal with the pain of the dissension.

Building bridges and creating a support system with family and friends is critical to mental health. Trauma induced by dissenting relationships is very real—and an enemy to the type of physical, spiritual, and mental wellness that we seek. Be aware of the support systems available to you in times of friction and stress.

The Apostle Paul likened the church to a human body. When one member suffers, we all suffer; when one rejoices, we all celebrate. When two members experience mental distress with one another, don't take sides in joining the battling parties. Rather, seek ways to bond with others for support and to ease the pressure.

Prayer

O God, when jealousies and rivalries veer their evil heads while families are grieving, instill in each family member a conciliatory bond of trust and support to buffer the mental anguish being experienced.

Encourage each member to develop mental, spiritual, and physical wellness to overcome the stress of the dissension so that the family body might be united in its common grief.

We pray in Jesus Name.

Amen.

CHAPTER SIX

A Time to Plant and
a Time to Pluck What Has Been Planted

(Ecclesiastes 3:2)

A Time to Plant

Though space limited us from having a large garden at the parsonage, my father cultivated his own "farm" on a church member's land not far from our home in Harrisburg, PA. Art, known as a chronic alcoholic, welcomed us regularly to plant, cultivate and harvest an overabundance of fresh tomatoes and vegetables.

As a child, I was also quite successful at planting my own pot of green beans. My attempts at growing watermelons did not go as well; neither did my efforts with the "money tree" that I planted. As a child, I had a reputation of being quite gullible. Someone convinced me that if I planted a simple severed branch of a tree and watered it that the next morning dollar bills would appear on the tips. The theory proved to be false, and I did not become rich overnight. Nevertheless, I found great joy in cultivating plants, reading seed catalogs and dreaming about what I might harvest.

In the summer of my sophomore year in high school—after we moved across the Susquehanna River to Camp Hill to purchase a house—I decided to buy two dwarf pear trees and an apricot tree, similar to the ones I had seen in Grandma Daisy's yard long before. I watched the two trees grow with delight. Sadly, when I returned from West Berlin in the summer of 1980. I discovered that my beautiful fruit trees had been chopped down.

In the backyards of both my childhood homes, my father had cultivated rose bushes. One encircled an arbor over the back gate to our home in Harrisburg, while others climbed ladder-like structures. Annually, he took pictures of us as children dressed in our Easter finery in front of his rose bushes. A couple blocks away, he photographed us at Italian Lake in front of the red and yellow tulip gardens each spring. On special occasions, he adorned us with fragrant corsages to match our formal finery.

ACTION STEP #3:

Take Time to Tend the Environment

It has been within our God-given nature to tend and till the earth from the very beginning of creation. Genesis 2:15 reads "The Lord God took the man and put him in the garden of Eden to till it and keep it." Since the very beginning of humanity, men and women have naturally found fulfillment farming and gardening.

The gentle rhythm of the cycle of planting and reaping brings a sense of peace. It can provide precious relief from the mental anguish that is sometimes experienced in our personal lives.

As I observed my father pastor to Art, the alcoholic, while planting tomatoes on his farm plot, I saw the healing power of his gentle pastoral guidance as they worked together

Andrew Boyer planting a tree for Habitat Work Day at Nixon Park, York, PA, in April, 2024.

staking up tomatoes and cultivating the garden. This was noticeably therapeutic for Art. The exact nature of Art's problems were unknown to me, but I did know as a child was that he had marital difficulties with his wife as well as many chronic alcoholic and psychiatric problems.

Engagement with Mother Earth can be the most satisfying therapy in coping with mental health issues. There is great joy in digging one's hands into the dark, rich earth, watering the seedlings, and watching each little sprout push its head above the ground, while meditating on the beauty of all creation. Remember to take time to tend the environment.

Prayer

O God, thank you for forming us in your image as caretakers of the beauty around us as we plant seeds and bulbs.

Help us to cultivate them with care and to let go of the pains within us, as we are inspired by the growth that abounds.

In Jesus' name we pray.

Amen.

A Time to Pluck Up What Has Been Planted

In mid-July of 2023, I was weary. I was experiencing numerous side effects from a drug I had began taking in March. I came to a new realization that I must strongly advocate for my own personal health. I would have to rise above my innate feeling of defeat, and speak out to address my mental heath issues and concerns.

More than two decades previously, I remembered similarly feeling very fatigued by a mixture of three types of medicines. When I told the doctors back then how badly I felt, they refused to make adjustments to my prescriptions. I suffered through years of over-medication until we moved and I consulted a new doctor who immediately changed my medications.

Though I am not a medical doctor, my experience has taught me that the wrong medications and over-medication can cause depression and other side effects. Well-meaning doctors then mistake these side effects as a symptoms of one's disease.

My July, 2023, symptoms caused me to fear that my medical history was repeating itself, but this time I found the courage to complain to the doctor and insist that he take my concerns seriously. He did a blood test and began changing my medicine immediately.

While we count on our family members for support during issues with medication, there is no substitute for self-advocacy in direct communication with our doctors. Those who experience mental illness must question the numerous side-effects of medication. Such suffering is not necessarily a given. It can be very difficult to muster the resolve to assert oneself and question medical treatment, but doing so is essential to find out what works best for *you*.

ACTION STEP #4

Take Time to Pluck the Negativity

Each person's body chemistry is different, and what works for one individual may not work for another. Today, there are numerous and better alternatives available than what were available when I first experienced my mental health issues. A change in diet and exercise are also known to help. But finding the right combination of strategies can feel overwhelming—or even impossible when you are suffering!

Overcoming negative feelings, communicating symptoms, and taking control of one's own care are all key to mental wellness. In addition to feeling helpless, those plagued by a mental illness frequently face feelings of shame, guilt and unworthiness. When these feelings abound, it is important to confide in a counselor to identify and address them. These negative feelings must be plucked up and discarded just as positive ones must be harvested.

Self-advocacy also plays an important role in finding what works. A psychiatrist cannot address symptoms that they do not know exist. Further, a patient must insist on finding a treatment that is appropriate for his or her symptoms and personal situation.

I find hope in a passage from Paul in Hebrews 12:11: "For the moment all discipline seems painful rather than pleasant, but later it yields the peaceful fruit of righteousness to those who have been trained by it." Though what we must endure to fight mental health challenges may be painful now, look forward to the harvest of peaceful fruit that is to come at the end of the struggle!

Prayer

O God, when I am down on myself, feeling bad about injury that I have caused or have suffered, or even the pains that I have inflicted upon myself, empower me with self-discipline.

Help me pluck out all traces of negativity so that I might once again rejoice in the harvest of peaceful fruit that is growing within me.

I pray in Jesus Name.

Amen.

Richard Butkofsky (brother) in a happy moment at the beach in August, 1991, less than a year before his suicide.*

CHAPTER SEVEN

A Time to Kill and a Time to Heal

(Ecclesiastes 3:3)

A Time to Kill

It was during the tumultuous years of the 1960's that I was confronted with the reality of horrible political killings and racial violence. I had just turned 10 years old when President John F. Kennedy was assassinated on November 22, 1963. The principal announced over the loudspeaker in our fifth-grade classroom at Steele Elementary School in Harrisburg that Kennedy had been shot. I was shocked. I denied it could be the President of the United States that been killed. "No, it must have been the governor of Texas!" The 1968 assassinations of Robert Kennedy and Martin Luther King, Jr., followed when I was a sophomore at William Penn High School, and these deaths had an even greater impact upon me. I was older and I had just become aware of the political turmoil and strife dividing our country. As a child, I knew that these killings were willful acts of violence that were against the Ten Commandments, but I had only begun to understand the complexity of the political situations in which these assassins acted. I began to accept the fact that killing was a part of life.

The most profound impact of these was the assassination of the Rev. Dr. Martin Luther King, Jr., on April 4, 1968. My parents had previously traveled by bus to Washington to march with Dr. King. They had invited me to go along, and I declined. When the racial riots of 1968 broke out in our high school, I did not understand what was happening. I just wondered why my best black friends that I had known since elementary school were not talking with me and, instead, were rushing to secret meetings in the school auditorium that were for blacks only. My brother, Richard, arrived home from school severely beaten and terrorized, having been beaten by a gang on the street. A youth slammed his trombone case on his back to beat him and blackened his eyes. This incident was the trigger of my brother's lifelong struggle with schizophrenia, which ended with his suicide at the age of 34.

An awful nightmare woke me up the night of the school riot. My initial impulse was to start looking in the newspaper for a new home that would be safe. My parents were also ready to move out of the parsonage to the more peaceful schools across the Susquehanna River in Camp Hill. Eventually, I changed my mind as I realized I would lose my childhood friends and no longer be able to fulfill my dream of graduating from William Penn High School. In contrast, my parents' decision to move to Camp Hill was firm.

They had an additional motivation for the change: my father was aging, and they wanted to move out of the church parsonage and purchase a home of their own. Though I pleaded with my parents to stay in Harrisburg, we were one of the many families in my school that left because of the race riots.

When our family weighed the pros and cons of this move, it seemed to make sense. In the case of my brother Richard, however, the move to Camp Hill did not eradicate his mental health issues. While adjusting to our new school, he continued to have traumatic episodes and prescription drug overdoses. For him, a later move to a boarding school to complete his high school education proved effective. My parents enrolled Richard in Mercersburg Academy, where he had greater supervision and eventually graduated.

ACTION STEP #5

Take Time to Make Major Life Changes

Sometimes the situations in which we find ourselves become so traumatic that a major change is necessary. It may be a new job, a different community, or even a reconfiguration of our family. Change is not the first alternative to a difficult situation. Yet the need for a fresh start sometimes becomes the only viable solution, providing new personal connections and an environment free of stress and debilitating memories.

As a pastor of 45 years, I moved nine times. Each move offered me a fresh start. I could draw upon what I had learned from prior experiences and put down roots in a new locale. Though each change was positive, it was not made without careful planning to become reestablished in the new locale. This process involved establishing a support system that included both psychiatric and collegiate resources. Well in advance of each move, I made contact with local physicians, counselors, and clergy support groups who helped tease the transition. Also, indispensable was the loving support of my husband, David, and son, Andrew, who settled us into our "new" homes each time we moved.

Prayer

O God, when the trauma within our immediate environment becomes pervasive, help us to deal with the difficult question, "Is it time to make a change?"

Calm our minds from the fears that this may create within us.

Help us weigh the pros and cons of whether to stay or to move!

Hear our prayer, O Lord, and grant us your peace.

In Jesus name we pray.

Amen.

A Time to Heal

Physical wellness was an important emphasis of my early years. President Kennedy instituted a national physical fitness program for young persons in the 1960s that included fitness standards. The physical education teacher in our school regularly timed us in the 50-yard dash. Each time our names and times were announced from best to worst in the class, I would shrink in embarrassment as my name was regularly last on the list. Similarly, the names of those completing a high number of push-ups and sit-ups were celebrated, while I felt ashamed that I could only push or pull my body up just once.

At home, physical wellness was also highly valued. Mother was a life-long nutrition advocate who lectured her three children on the "do's-and-don'ts" of dieting. Her high school yearbook mentioned she would be seeking a career in nutrition, yet her undergraduate degree from Ursinus College was in history and teacher education.

Weighing just 118 pounds at her wedding, Mother instilled in me great anxiety that at 130 pounds I was a grossly overweight teen. She enrolled each of us in YWCA ballet classes at age 7 and shortly afterwards encouraged us to participate in a swimming program. The pattern for family dinners was very strict; we did not eat till the dinner bell rang.

I often begged her for coins to drop in the vending machines at the swimming pool. At home, I complained of hunger pangs and discreetly raided the cookie jar. Ultimately, I became obsessive watching my weight.

Father also focused upon physical fitness. Early in his life, he often hiked parts of the Appalachian Trail. He led youth groups hiking on the Trail and encouraged ice skating events well into his sixties. When I was a teen and he was in his seventies, he continued to walk the neighborhood surrounding our home.

Our Sunday School lessons often focused upon the body as the temple of the Holy Spirit our church regularly had charismatic healing services. I attended prayer services with my family at the Episcopal Church in Harrisburg and, while in college, charismatic services in Pittsburgh. I prayed that I might receive healing for my fluctuating weight problem. During my college years, I also sought miraculous healing via the services of Kathryn Kuhlman. This was the first of several experiences I have had seeking healing within worship.

ACTION STEP #6

Take Time to Write

As I continued my quest for Shalom, I discovered that writing brought me closer to the treasured peace that I sought. Upon returning from Turkey, I had a very poor self-image regarding my body and my mental health. I joined

Overeaters Anonymous and followed its 12-Step Program. I identified with those who described themselves as compulsive overeaters. Sugar cravings and my effort to satisfy them made my weight fluctuate excessively. Engaging in the 12-Step Program with a sponsor helped me to reflect on my life, especially writing an inventory of my life. Besides losing weight, I experienced deep spiritual healing—dealing with issues that had troubled me since adolescence. I began to incorporate Reinhold Niebuhr's famous Serenity Prayer into my life, "God, grant me serenity to accept the things I cannot change, the courage to change the things I can, and the wisdom to know the difference."

When I wrote my personal inventory for the 12-step program, I discovered that the tool of writing comforted me and helped heal me spiritually. Though I no longer am involved with the 12-Step Program, I continue to find spiritual wellness in writing.

I write letters and devotionals each day and will continue to write them until my mind ceases to function. I wrote my first letter as a child from Camp Michaux, a United Church of Christ church camp. For my trip, my father had packed stationery and a self-addressed stamped envelope in my rucksack with the instruction that was to write home during the middle of the week. I followed his instructions, and I have been writing letters ever since.

The process of writing can be very uplifting. We can feel the words transfer from what I call "creative migraines" through our fingertips to the paper or screen. When the transfer is complete, we can see the results. If our self-expression is just right, it instills in us a warm, satisfying sense of Shalom.

Prayer

O God, as I write down my innermost thoughts, relieve the spiritual migraines in my soul.

Move my thoughts from within my brain through my fingertips to the page.

And may these pages bring spiritual relief not only to me, but to others who may read what I have written, so that our lives might be bettered through the writing of these humble expressions.

Amen.

Martha, Andrew, and David on a restful cruise on her sabbatical in St. Louis, Missouri, in July, 1999.

CHAPTER EIGHT

A Time to Break Down and a Time to Build

(Ecclesiastes 3:3)

A Time to Break Down

Mildred Rupp, an elderly single lady, was a long-time member and regular attendee of Salem UCC; to us Butkofsky children, she was our primary babysitter. My parents picked her up each week for church services. Midge was practically a member of our family. I was deeply disturbed when I was 19 years old and Midge confronted me with the question: "Are you having a breakdown? People in the church are saying that you are having a breakdown?"

I broke into tears not because I was having a breakdown, but merely because I was deeply hurt by the suspicion that I was. At the time, I felt confident and mentally healthy, but I was aware of the great stigma surrounding mental illness. I felt burdened by the weight of shame associated with it.

Looking back, I now understand the reason for the gossip. My brother Richard had had several psychotic episodes. In addition, my older sister Karen had had problems in her senior year and remained at home for a year between high school and college. She had found healing through the ministry of a new church. As a preacher's kid who was extremely sensitive to gossip about my family and living in what felt like a goldfish bowl, I understand the reason for the gossip.

There was some history of mental illness and alcoholism on my father's side of the family about which my mother often spoke. She denied there was any mental illness on her side of the family. I was also deeply stressed by my relationship with my mother during the time Richard had his psychotic episodes in our home. I requested a counseling session with my mother to work on my relationship with her.

Living with the fear that something similar would happen to me and unable to resolve the issues between my mother and myself, my coping strategy was to seek employment near Carnegie-Mellon University in Pittsburgh during my college summers. My high school summers away from home at Chautauqua Music School also provided a welcome respite.

At the age of 26 and before I left for Turkey, I was cleared medically by the doctor at the United Church Board for World Ministries (UCBWM) in New York City. Yet, less than six months later—as I have described earlier in this book—I was sent home on a medical furlough having had a psychotic episode in Istanbul.

Dr. Herbert Cooper, III, first described my breakdown as a chemical imbalance with a diagnosis code "Schizophreniform disorder in remission," and he described it as hereditary. This was the first of many attempts to diagnosis the trauma that I had first experienced in Istanbul. He was unable to tell me during the first year of treatment whether I would ever have another episode. But he did tell me at our first meeting in January, 1981, that he needed to treat me for one year to be certain a similar episode would not occur in the future. At the end of the year, I was off medication, symptom-free, and Dr. Cooper dismissed me. With my medical furlough ended, the UCBWM encouraged me to apply for another position overseas, but I did not feel ready. Instead, I sought employment as a pastor in the US, where I would be close to doctors if I had similar medical symptoms.

ACTION STEP #7:

Take Time to Understand and to Be Understood

One of the most difficult challenges of living with mental health issues is isolation. When I experience a psychotic episode, I am transported into another world and I am unable to make contact with the real world—unaware of what is actually happening. Those who have experienced this state will agree that living in Hell could be no worse.

Upon exiting an episode, we discover we have had blackouts—periods of which we have no memory. It takes a great deal of time to process what has happened. Relationships with others may have changed because of the episode. We need help from family, friends, and counselors to fill in the blank spots and comprehend what has happened. Understanding and patience from those around us is essential as we may be ashamed of how we behaved. With an acceptance of what we have experienced, however, there can be both relief and gratitude that we were treated, even though we may never recall the details of the episodes.

Understanding what we have been through with the help of compassionate family, friends, and counselors brings a sense of Shalom. Their eyes and ears witness our episodes and later help us to piece together the missing pieces in the puzzle of our trauma. This process may take several months; in my case, the process took several decades until I was willing to do the actual work of *seeking to understand and to be understood*. That is, admitting the severity of the trauma.

St. Francis of Assisi famously prayed, "Lord, make me an instrument of thy peace…. O Divine Master, grant that I may not so much seek to be understood as to understand." To become an instrument of God's peace, we must seek first, as Francis says, *understanding*; but to arrive toward a true peace, we also need to be *understood*. As I continue my quest for Shalom, I find peace as I not only understand myself, but as I am compassionately understood by others.

Prayer

O God, sometimes our bodies break down and we become entrapped in nightmare.

Sometimes our realities are difficult to comprehend.

Sometimes our relationships are strained due to circumstances outside of our control.

Grant us the courage to face the unknown and the incomprehensible episodes of our lives so that we might better understand who we are.

Then give us the patience and the fortitude of relationships to be understood by others, so that compassionate understanding and peace may be provoked in our psyches.

In Jesus' name we pray.

Amen.

A Time to Build

The time to break down had passed; now was my time to build.

My first step was to move out of my missionary furlough residence at Lancaster Seminary. I needed an apartment and a car. I also wanted a job so I would not be dependent on my missionary furlough income. Soon, I located a furnished efficiency apartment that was $150 per month. I was beginning to reemerge with my independence. My sister Karen had a "friend" who sold me a 1968 red Volkswagen Bug. She taught me how to navigate the stick shift in a Harrisburg cemetery. I am certain the folks were rising from their graves as that little red bug stalled and shook among the tombstones!

One day the phone rang with news of an angel coming to visit me; the angel's name was Jens Rüggeberg from Tübingen, West Germany. Horace Sills at the Penn Central Conference called to tell me Jens was coming to the United States to visit me. Jens and I had met at a peace conference on the Wahnsee Lake in West Berlin at the old Goebbels' Estate (named for Paul Joseph Goebbel's, close confident of Adolf Hitler and chief propagandist for the Nazi Party).

After my initial meeting with Jens in West Berlin, I hitchhiked ten hours by truck to visit Jens and his roommates at Tübingen University, where Jens studied law. Jens had planned to visit me in Istanbul over Spring Break. When he heard that I was back in the United States, he changed his itinerary to visit me in Lancaster, Pennsylvania. Jens helped me load my belongings into my red bug at Lancaster Seminary and, then helped me move into the efficiency apartment which would to be my home for the next year. For a month, Jens and I played tourists in Lancaster. He was fascinated with the Amish and the

Ephrata Cloister. I enjoyed touring these sights that I had neglected to see while growing up in Harrisburg. This was more than a time of healing; it was a time that allowed me to rebuild my confidence and spirits.

Jens' future ambition was to live in a commune in Israel. On the very last day of his visit, he said as he departed, "Martha let's not kid ourselves" meaning that our time together had a very precious but transitory purpose. He left that day for the airport with his rucksack, but all he left behind was his hiking shoes. That was the last time I saw Jens Ruggeberg. Sometimes I wonder if somewhere in Israel he is alive, thriving in a kibbutz.

By the summer of 1981, I was working in telephone and home sales for United Publishers. I joined the choir at St. Peter's United Church of Christ in Lancaster and was seeking placement as a pastor in the United Church of Christ. By the end of the year, I was stable without medication and had been discharged as a patient of Dr. Cooper.

But my mental health turned out not to be as stable as I had hoped. In May, 1982, I was once again feeling an awful weight of stress upon my limbs. I walked to the Emergency Room at Lancaster General—just a block from my efficiency apartment—and admitted myself. My admittance was immediate, and I was placed in a private room at the hospital.

When I could not go to sleep that night, I walked down the hallway to the nurses' station and collapsed. The staff helped me back to my bed, and I was given a low dose of Mellaril—a medication I had taken previously—and my recovery was rapid. I resumed therapy with Dr. Cooper; my hospitalization was just five days. In fact, the doctor gave me special permission to leave the hospital daily during my stay so I could continue working.

Still, this relapse mortified me. Was I going to have to live with this for life? Would I have to remain on medication forever? Would I be handicapped and face the same debilitating future that my brother Richard struggled with for so many years?

I decided to keep this episode a secret. I did not want to have lengthy discussions because of my discomfort with the subject. I feared being labeled "mentally ill."

The same evening I was discharged from the hospital and back home in my apartment, I received a phone call from the Search Committee at First United Church of Christ in Warren, Ohio. They invited me to have a phone interview followed by a visit to Warren for a trial sermon. The congregation would then vote to elect me as their pastor. I was shocked by the sudden invitation. So shocked that I really did not know how to say no! I said "Yes," and made plans to fly to Youngstown, Ohio.

One month later, I was elected as their pastor and moved to Warren, Ohio. I arranged a local therapist to counsel me during the transition and prescribe medication. I also contacted the local clergy groups to provide the peer support that I needed in the transition to my first sole pastorate, where I met another "angel," Rev. James Haun, who was also beginning a new pastorate in Eastern Ohio. He later quipped of beginning his first call as a pastor:

I entered my office on the first day of my work as Pastor, sat behind my new desk and looked over it and exclaimed, "Now what do I do?"

Telling this anecdote, all the new clergy hearing it burst out laughing. But in that laughter, I realized that I was not the only one with a sense of terror at the weighty prospect of living into the high calling of being a pastor.

When my mother arrived in Warren to help me settle into my apartment, we had a heart-to-heart talk—a first for the two of us. I told her I wanted to go "home," but I had no permanent home base. It wasn't my mother's house in Camp Hill, the Lancaster Seminary, or my Lancaster apartment. Neither was it the places I had lived in New York City, Pittsburgh, Costa Rica, or Istanbul. Since leaving for college in 1971, my most permanent residence had been the place I had lived for almost two years in West Berlin. I had no real home where I could return. I longed for a permanent address and another chance at ministry. Looming over me was my first meeting with the church's consistory (board) that night, and I asked my mother not to leave until after I would see how that first meeting went. Despite my fears, I was warmly welcomed by the Consistory at my first meeting, and my nervous hesitation at taking on the task of pastor dissipated.

Returning from the first consistory meeting, I went back to my apartment and told my mother she could go home; the meeting went well, and I would be staying in Ohio.

Another clergy colleague told me this helpful advice about new beginnings:

Listen to them and love them, and you will learn on-the-job training about how to be a pastor, and learn the necessary things that you did not learn in seminary.

With the support of the therapist, a clergy group, and the understanding of loving people of the First United Church of Christ in Warren, Ohio, I began to learn what it was to be their pastor.

ACTION STEP #8

Take Time for Reinvigorating Rest and Recreation

Eighteen years later, after twenty years of ordained ministry and seven years serving as Pastor of Christ Church United Church of Christ, I was granted a sabbatical of 3 months for rest, reflection, and further education. This "stop" on my quest for Shalom energized me for the next twenty-five years of ministry.

As pastors, we need to be examples for our congregation on what it means to follow the fourth commandment, "Remember the Sabbath and keep it holy." For those of us who are mentally health-challenged, observing this commandment is even more vital for our wellness. We need to take one day a week for rest and thanksgiving. for spiritual things to avert health crisis. I learned that my Sabbath rest had to be on a day other than my Sunday workday. A time of spiritual refreshment and renewal with the Lord should be a priority, not an occasional event. In addition, we need extended times of rest like the sabbatical I took in 1999 after seven years of ministry at Christ Church. This was one of two sabbaticals that I was granted during my 45 years of ministry.

During my first 20 years of ordained ministry, I had averted episodes through counseling and low-dose medication. My support systems were strong as in each location I had participated in collegian networks. My Achilles Heel, however, was the strong-ingrained Protestant work ethic, which drove me to fill in every blank spot on my calendar.

As the pastor of a 200+ member church which averaged about 100 for Sunday worship, I was typical of many other clergy: I worked long hours for many years without relief. It was difficult to draw appropriate boundaries between our work and our personal lives. Christ Church, United Church of Christ, supported me in my efforts for further education in a Doctor of Ministry Program at Lancaster Theological Seminary, providing me with the necessary spiritual refreshment to deal with the challenges of long-term ministry. My three-month sabbatical for rest and reflection coincided with writing my Doctor of Ministry dissertation, which was an important "stop" on my quest for Shalom.

During the sabbatical in 1999, David, Andrew, and I traveled throughout the United States, in a small fifth-wheel coast-to-coast, 10,901 miles. I had a true rest from the daily tasks of being a pastor as I pursued a real learning quest of my own design. Wearied by the fluctuations in worship attendance and anxieties about death of congregations in urban neighborhoods, I sought peace of mind by studying churches that had revitalized after almost dying. I studied United Church of Christ Congregations across the nation which had almost died and then revitalized in worship attendance. Clearly these churches were in the minority in mainline denominations in the 1990s.

This self-structured sabbatical allowed me to have a true rest from my pastoral setting and find something that was invigorating, restful, and adventuresome for me and my family. From the research of this sabbatical, I published my dissertation in 2000, *Turnabout from the Low Ebb: A Study of How Mid-sized Churches in Urban Transitional Neighborhoods have Effected Turnabouts in Worship Attendance.*[1] Within the book were case studies of churches that had almost died but had been revitalized.

As I learned their stories of revitalization, I became rested and revitalized as well. On my sabbaticals, I discovered Action Step #8, that is, to take time for reinvigorating rest and recreation.

Prayer

O God, sometimes we spin non-stop on the "hamster wheel of life" at work and at home.

Sometimes we push forward, over-pressured and saddened by declining numbers in attendance.

Put on the brakes for us, that we may slow our pace and stop to rest.

Help us to find refreshment and even to break out of the cages in which we find ourselves entrapped.

When we return to the spinning wheel of our work, guide us to do so with a renewed and steadied pace keeping centered upon the mission you have called us.

We pray in Jesus' Name.

Amen.

Martha and Andrew laughing as they polka dance at the Manchester, PA, fire department in October, 2023.

CHAPTER NINE

A Time to Weep and a Time to Laugh

(Ecclesiastes 3:3)

When I awoke in my Istanbul hospital bed, I felt numbness in my limbs and I was bewildered as to what had happened to me. I walked over to the mirror and just stared at my face. I had an overpowering urge to weep, but was unable to do so—likely the result of the heavy dose of medication in my body. It would not be until early one morning 40 years later, as I began to recall the details of what had happened to me for a class project, that I finally had a really good cry. I wept about what had happened, and those tears were healing.

I do not have much to write about my experience of weeping. Growing up, I was taught one does not cry! I remember hearing, "Don't be a crybaby!" Through I was told this, I could still relate to the very human feeling of needing to weep,

I held back tears in public—preferring a private cry. Such was the case when I experienced the loss of my grandparents. Likewise, I held my tears when I felt I was being unfairly punished, anguished by the suffering of others, or simply watching a sad movie. I wanted to cry all alone.

While expressing these emotions in public was not condoned by my parents, they did encourage me to find other outlets to express my deepest feelings—acting and singing. I was involved in school and community theater productions. There is a wholesome release of emotions when we become wrapped up in the pathos of the characters we are portraying. Those of us who have experienced theater as actors have heightened emotions as we watch others act out the characters.

I also developed a great fondness for tragic operas such as *La Boheme, Madame Butterfly, Norma, Carmen,* and *I Pagliacci*. The latter is the story of a clown who paints his face with a smile while inside his broken heart is weeping. Listening to the lyrics of the operas, I could emotionally experience the pathos of these tragic figures.

ACTION STEP #9

Take Time to Weep

It is truly a blessing to be able to weep. In a *Harvard Health Blog,* Leo Newhouse identifies crying as a phenomenon unique to humans. He continues by writing that crying

> is a natural response to a range of emotions, from deep sadness and grief to extreme happiness and joy. But is crying good for your health? The answer appears to be yes. Medical benefits of crying have been known as far back as the Classical era. Thinkers and physicians of ancient Greece and Rome posited that tears work like a purgative, draining off and purifying us. Today's psychological thought largely concurs, emphasizing the role of crying as a mechanism that allows us to release stress and emotional pain.[1]

Crying while watching dramatic presentations, that is, sad television shows or movies, might sound counterintuitive to feeling better. But from a psychological perspective, according to Nancy Sokarno, "Consuming depressing content can actually make you feel good [because] of [increased] endorphins." When we want to watch a sad movie in congruence with how sad we are, "our brains are essentially chasing those feel good endorphins."[2]

As we take time to cry, we are blessed with empathy, connection, and awareness of social relations. These are all signs of emotional wellness.

Prayer

O God:

Draw me out of myself into another world, be it fantasy or non-fiction, where I can focus the intensity of my feelings on the emotions of others and myself from the awful ache that is trapped inside me.

Allow me to transfer the burden of my inner brokenness on some object outside of myself and find relief in the unleashing of internal wretchedness.

Above all, help me to find refuge in the suffering and cross of Jesus Christ, my Savior, who truly provided the ultimate outlet for my mental pain and anguish as he lifts me up with him through his holy resurrection.

In Christ's name we pray.

Amen.

A Time to Laugh

Lest this book turn into a series of laments bemoaning my mental handicap, I now reflect upon the attitude of Proverbs 17:22: "A cheerful heart is a good medicine, but a crushed spirit dries up the bones." I want my heart to be a cheerful one that provides good medicine to folk, rather than drying up their spirits. I want the description of my illness to only be a single lament within the midst of the broader context of my life's story.

How can this book be of help to anyone else suffering from the challenges of mental illness if it is simply an expression of self-pity or a plea for sympathy? Dr. Cooper, my first psychiatrist, told me at one of my first appointments that I should be grateful to have this medical condition and not diabetes, which is far more debilitating and can cause loss of limbs and lifelong dietary issues. The treatment for my condition is a correction of an imbalance of chemicals within my body. My positive, lucid moments have far out-lengthened the traumatic brief episodes. The joy that I experience in laughter trumps the awful ache of mental anguish.

Throughout the years I have experienced a variety of significantly joyful relationships too numerous to mention. Being an extrovert, a linguist, well-traveled and quite verbose, I have talked with people all over the world in a variety of languages. I have not been embarrassed making mistakes in attempting to speak, because the only way to become fluent in a language is to speak the language! I love to make linguistic jokes. I am not sure if my *amigos* and *Freunden* (friends) found them funny or not, but we all laughed wholeheartedly.

Once I presented an early morning devotional for a confirmation retreat at a guest house in Münster. I used Cat

Steven's "Morning Has Broken" for the opening song. I translated the song into German as *"Morgen hat gebrochen,"* which literally means "morning has vomited." The youth burst out laughing. Then I said, "Sometimes you feel like that in the morning." They thought I had made a common mistranslation when the correct translation would have been, *"Morgen ist erbrochen."*

ACTION STEP #10

Take Time to Laugh
(to Develop a Sense of Humor)

One of the most difficult challenges during mental health episodes is recovering a good sense of humor. Just as peace can come to those who learn to laugh at themselves, a special sense of healing comes when we are able to finally accept the humor of the delusions we have experienced and even laugh about them. Be grateful for your sense of humor, but don't use it to hurt or embarrass either yourself or others.

To develop a great sense of humor, be aware of your environment, what you are reading and with whom you are surrounding yourself. We can find "communities of laughter" in choirs, at church meetings, and most importantly in the communities in which we reside, among family and friends. If there is a lack of laughter in these settings, then amuse yourself with stand-up comediennes and from multi-media and books. We cannot reach a true sense of Shalom without developing an authentic sense of humor, even silliness.[3]

Prayer

O God,

Tickle my funny bone and massage my spirit so I may find the humor in life that will relieve the pressure and anxiety.

Help me find ways to transform the seriousness of life into celebration of merriment.

Transform my inward preoccupation with paranoia into an outward observation of the amusements of life.

Instill me with holy humor, that will disarm the drudgery of dealing with the constant stress of mental health issues

Thank you for the peace which this spirit of merriment brings to us.

In Jesus name we pray.

Amen.

CHAPTER TEN

A Time to Mourn and a Time to Dance

(Ecclesiastes 3:4)

A Time to Mourn

A scene in James Michener's *Hawaii* relates the story of a native mourning the loss of his wife, who was also his sister, by gouging out his eyes. There are Bible stories of people beating their chests at funerals. A story in the Hebrew Bible tells of the city of Nineveh: "Beauty is stripped, she is carried away; her ladies-in-waiting moan like the sound of doves and beat their breasts" (Nahum 2:7). In the New Testament we are told that after the crucifixion of Jesus many went away beating their breasts (Luke 23:48).

Contemplating a "time to mourn" is different than considering "a time to die." Death does not always bring mourning and sometimes offers relief. Mourning seeks relief. It is when we sense a tightening and aching in our chest from a deep loss that can often be only alleviated by beating our breasts with our fists.

I first became aware of what it means to mourn when I was a 9-year-old mourning the loss of my beloved black cat, Cola. Using all my developing maternal instincts, I had cared for her as my "baby," There is a special attachment that we have to our pets who become like children, held and stroked and fed utterly dependent on us for care. I was surprised that I felt more sadness when Cola died that I had felt at my grandmother's funeral years earlier. I had more feline pets throughout my teenage years: Oreo, Kitty and

Buffet; I grieved the loss of each one. After we were married, David and I had other cats, dogs, birds, and fish. We mourned each as they passed.

Our first and only dog was our son Andrew's dog, Shakespeare. Since the third grade when I had been chased by a stray on the way to school, I had a deep fear of being bitten by a rabid dog. Since then, I have avoided dogs. Shakespeare was part of a plea bargain with Andrew to move to Macungie, Pennsylvania. Andrew was grieving the loss of friends and school when we left Jonestown to move to Macungie. As we were planning our move, David and I offered to lessen Andrew's "pain" by getting him a dog. Shortly after our move, Andrew got his dog—a beige Cairn Terrier named Shakespeare.

Shakespeare was protective of his ball and food. He became snappy and aggressive when anyone attempted to intervene with his play or meal. Still, we learned to love him with all of his quirks. He became a part of our family and joined us for dinner daily, though he was not allowed to eat any food till after our family prayer.

With time, Shakespeare developed a number of health issues. When he developed a chronic skin affliction, Andrew gave him a medicated bath each week. At the age of 13, Shakespeare developed pancreatitis, became diabetic and was blind. We administered his daily insulin shots and eyes drops. Late one Sunday night he passed, just a few feet away from my feet on a La-Z-Boy chair.

A marble table in our dining room with his ashes, ball, kerchief, paw prints and muzzle serves as our memorial to him. The Christmas after Shakespeare died, we purchased a look-alike stuffed clone that was fabricated in the likeness of Shakespeare. But four years later, we continue to mourn the loss of our beloved Shakespeare.

On Earth Day, 2013, I was serving as Pastor at St. Paul United Church of Christ in Shrewsbury, Pennsylvania. Each member of the congregation was given a shoot of a dogwood tree to take home and plant. David, Andrew and I planted our "Tree of Hope" on the edge of the apartment complex where we lived. We have watched this dogwood tree grow and flower year since; Each year we visit the tree on Thanksgiving Day and celebrate a ritual of thanksgiving and remembrance. When Shakespeare was alive, we took him with us. Now, we take along his clone. This is one of the rituals of celebration that we perform as we continue to mourn the loss of Shakespeare.

ACTION STEP #11

Take Time for Funerals

Part of the mourning process are funeral rituals, which help alleviate the awful ache of loss. As a pastor for 45 years, I regularly officiated funerals. On All Saint's Day, I have also led congregations in this annual remembrance of those who have passed during the year—lighting candles and ringing the church bell to recognize each individual's death.

Whether referred to as a funeral, memorial service, or celebration of life, these rituals are usually quite traditional including scriptures and the story of the deceased person's life and family situation. It is difficult to say one ever becomes an expert at funerals, but it is certain one never become callous to the human mourning at the time of death. Being sensitive to those who are mourning enables one to be truly present for them in their grief and allows the Holy Spirit to move in a very special way.

Andrew and Martha with Carrie Sierra and Clone of Shakespeare at our Tree of Hope in November, 2023.

As mentally health challenged individuals participate in meaningful rituals honoring those who have passed, we are given the space and a supportive community that helps us cry and deal with our own deep losses, even if it is not just primarily the loss of the one whom we are honoring at that particular service. For in the loss of close family and friends, we also must face our own mental anguish and mortality. Often we find comfort in the fact that the physical pain and suffering has ended. We also might find hope in the resurrection to eternal life which is expressed in the eulogies and liturgies—not just for the deceased but for ourselves.

The process of mourning takes time and can't be rushed. Beware of trying to fill a void too quickly. We waited to get our new beloved cat, Carrie Sierra, for four years after our dog, Shakespeare, passed. One must also recognize it can take months, or even years, to absorb a loss and accept how life has changed. One may need to seek professional help." Acknowledging the need for and reaching out for such guidance is a sign of strength, not weakness. Throughout the process of mourning, with the help of memorial rituals and if need be, professional help, we can reach a resolution of Shalom.

Prayer

O God,

Teach us to mourn properly so that we may fully appreciate those we mourn.

Allow us to be kind and patient with ourselves and each other to fully feel the awful ache of our losses.

Help us to remember the very best of their lives that we might honor their memories.

Enable us to carry on their honored legacies among those left behind.

You have deemed us blessed who mourn, promising to comfort us.

Grant us the comfort of your peace, as we pray in Jesus' name.

Amen.

A Time to Dance

I began ballet lessons as a young child at the YWCA. Later, I participated in theater dance lessons. All of the Butkofsky children took ballroom dancing lessons at the Harrisburg Civic Club. I found joy in these experiences, but not from mimicking formalized steps but rather being able to express outwardly the joy I was feeling inwardly. Dance also provided relief from anxiety. In dancing, I did not seek perfection in form, but perfection in spirit.

I better understood the gift of dance as a young adult. In college, I was enamored by the movie *Fiddler on the Roof,* and I watched it over and over again. The film revealed such a natural expression of joy despite the harsh persecution experienced by the characters. Then, in 1969, I attended the International Camp on Mersea Island in East Essex, where I experienced the joy of this kind spontaneous dancing first-hand. Attendees from the Israeli delegation gathered outside their tent by campfire and performed a circle dance to *"Hava Nagila"* and other Israeli folk tunes. They invited me to clasp arms with them in the spirited dance.

I have since learned that in Hasidic Judaism, dance is a tool to express joy and it also has a deliberate therapeutic effect stimulating and expressing joy. Further, dancing is believed to purify the soul, promote spiritual elation, and unify a community.

My Union Seminary buddy Steve and I enjoyed freestyle disco dancing of the 1970s more than any rigid form of waltz, foxtrot, or tango. Which is probably why now I enjoy so much our "Shake Rattle and Roll Aqua Dance" classes at our local Jewish Community Center. We dance underwater with abandon matching not the form but the spirit of the instructor. My body receives a complete physical workout that also refreshes my mind and spirit. Like the other pairs contrasted in these verses from Ecclesiastes, "mourning" and "dancing" are somewhat outside of our control. They are a spontaneous reaction to human life, even though dancing is quite beautiful.

ACTION STEP #12

Take Time for Grounding Techniques

Dance and other forms of physical exercise often include repetitive motions that make us aware of our bodies and release tension: deep breaths, placing both feet flat on the floor, foot stomping, creating fists with one's hands, and clapping. Our bodies release endorphins within the brain and nervous system that have a number of physiological functions, including an analgesic effect creating a sense of well-being. Physical activity can also help a person "ground oneself"—providing a distraction from anxious feelings.

Waltzing, hiking, or marching, movement helps us to pace ourselves in rhythm with a normal average heart rate of 72 beats per minute. Waltzing, like learning any kind of dance, gets easier with practice. As the rhythmic pattern of these grounding techniques becomes more consistent, we become naturally more relaxed and joyful.

Prayer

O God:

When I feel lethargic and unable to get going, give me a gentle nudge to remove the inertia in my body.

As an object at rest tends to stay at rest, nudge me so that I may be an object in motion, pacing myself properly and continuing that motion.

Get me moving, O God, when I feel stuck in my lounge chair, unable to budge.

Motivate me to take just one step out of the chair and then another and then another and then another...

Help me ground myself so that the natural endorphins in my body are released, as I raise my arms high above, far below and all around.

I praise you, God, as now I feel so good.

In Jesus name, I pray.

Amen.

CHAPTER ELEVEN

A Time to Cast Away Stones, and a Time to Gather Stones Together

(Ecclesiastes 3:5)

"Throwing stones," as described in the book of Ecclesiastes, has been interpreted as the demobilization of military forces, just as the gathering of stones relates to the mobilization for war. While my denomination, the United Church of Christ, is not one of the traditional peace churches, it has passed several resolutions on peace and gun violence. At the 34th General Synod of the United Church of Christ, delegates passed a resolution on "Affirming Guns to Gardens and other Gun Violence Prevention Ministries." There is hope expressed in the statement that the symbols of aggression will be thrown away. Among other things the denomination resolved to host events to distribute gun safes and locks to promote the safe storage of firearms and prevent unauthorized accidental use.

During my teen years when I was distraught that both my family and the world seemed to be at war, I found much peace in singing, playing instruments and listening to music. I actually researched music therapy programs in Florida and New England as a possible career. A favorite song that I sang to myself was

> Sing, sing a song,
> make it simple
> to last your whole life long.
> Don't worry if it's not good enough
> for anyone else to hear
> just sing, sing a song.[1]

Pastors intuitively are musical therapists as they weave the liturgy and music together in the worship service to inspire praise, thanksgiving, faith and penitence. I have often quoted familiar songs and hymns within Sunday messages. While I was Pastor of St. Paul UCC in Shrewsbury, Pennsylvania, we typically closed the service with "Let there be Peace on Earth," "and let it begin with me."[2]

As a pastor, I often used this song and other worship music for their therapeutic value.

ACTION STEP #13

Take Time for Music

I never did major in music therapy, but I learned that music can be an effective remedy for depression. One starts with somber music matching one's mood. What follows is a gentle introduction of increasingly dynamic music that ultimately uplifts the person's disposition. In doing this of course, consideration must be given to an individual's musical taste and preferences.

The violent events of today's world can quickly create a sense of despair among persons susceptible to depression. Songs of peace and God's grace can provide comfort and hope. Music and song can motivate people to demobilize and find non-violent ways of resolving conflicts.

Music provided such comfort and hope for the African slaves in dealing with the oppression of slavery. They gathered to sing Spirituals in "praise houses" and outdoor "brush arbor meeting," "bush meetings," or "camp meetings" in the eighteenth century. According to the Library of Congress' preservation of these experiences, the

African slaves "would sing, chant, dance and sometimes enter ecstatic trances that were also sung on the plantations as they worked.... As Africanized Christianity took hold of the slave population, spirituals served as a way to express the community's new faith as well as its sorrows and hopes."[3]

Later during the 1960s, Spirituals such as "Down by the Riverside" and songs of freedom like "We Shall Overcome" served to unify and pacify rage and form non-violent protests against discrimination. Music not only serves us to cope with personal feelings of depression and sorrow, but is also a way enormous crowds can collectively express their protest.

Prayer

O God,

Thank you for the gift of music that soothes and uplifts our spirits.

May their melodies be etched in our memory banks to be resources of spiritual uplift on days we are low in spirit.

Thank you for the gift of lyrics set rhythmically to song to sustain us in life's journeys.

May we recall their counsel in moments of distress.

May they move us to higher ground when we aspire towards noble achievements.

Help the gentle tones bring us peace and inspire us.

We pray in Jesus' name.

Amen.

A Time to Gather Stones Together

As a pacifist, I find it hard to accept that there is a time to gather stones together, to prepare for war. The Ten Commandments have been so ingrained into my psyche that I find it difficult to accept there is a time for killing and murder. It is simply not meant to exist in a utopia, a world of peace and happiness. Yet it does exist as a part of the insanity in our world that God has created.

Growing up in the 1960s and 1970s, I am not blind to military conflict and its causes. The Vietnam War became increasingly unpopular with television newscasts in the later years as nightly newscasts were dominated by "casualty counts" and anti-war demonstrations. Soldiers were rarely given hero celebrations when they returned home.

My male college classmates were among the first who were unable to defer military service. In 1971, when many of us reached the age of 18, it was the year the US Congress reformed the military draft. Previously, a man could qualify for a student deferment if he could show he was a full-time student making satisfactory progress in virtually any field of study. He could continue to go to school and be deferred from service until he was too old to be drafted.

While women of my generation were not drafted, we did debate what we would do if we were enlisted. I was well aware that had I been of the opposite gender my draft number would have been a 10. My decision to not want to go into the military was not only due to fear of the senseless horrible violence on the battlefield, but also because I truly did not believe that I could initiate harm against another person for the reasons being used to defend that particular war.

Later, during the Cold War, when I lived in Germany on the west side of the Berlin Wall, there were constant reminders of Hitler's aggressive campaign against 6 million primarily Jewish victims and the horrors of the concentration camps. In the face of these atrocities, I sadly admit, as a pacifist, that there are times "to gather stones together."

During the 1960s, the war in southeast Asia was not the only conflict garnering much attention in the news In his first State of the Union Address (January, 1964) President Lyndon B. Johnson launched a "War on Poverty." With 20% of our nation's citizens considered poor at the time, President Johnson proclaimed he did not see this condition as a moral failure of an underclass but a failure of society: "The cause may lie deeper in our failure to give our fellow citizens a fair chance to develop their own capacities, in a lack of education and training, in a lack of medical care and housing, in a lack of decent communities in which to live and bring up their children."[4]

Fighting the root causes that hinder people from acquiring the basic necessities for living makes far more sense than going to battle against people because of ideological, cultural, or economic differences, particularly when one considers the lives and property destroyed as a consequence.

ACTION STEP #14

Take Time to Advocate for Wellness

Just as President Johnson declared war on poverty versus people, consider declaring war on other aspects of our lives that can benefit us. Declare war in other aspects that will benefit our lives rather than lead to detriment.

What if our energy and resources are spent on wellness? We need to advocate for such resources to be made available for everyone to participate in health and fitness centers. Seniors 65 and older are already eligible to participate free-of-charge in Silver Sneakers Programs, sponsored by some insurances and Medicare Advantage plans. I hold free membership in two health and fitness clubs through this Silver Sneakers Program: the Jewish Community Center (JCC) and the YMCA.

I have used the fitness center and the pool at the JCC since I turned 65. According to its website, "The York JCC creates opportunities for everyone, inspires relationships, builds a community of well-being, and enhances Jewish communal life. We aren't just a gym! From fitness, education, cultural to youth and aquatic opportunities. We provide a supportive, inclusive and welcoming environment. Our members call us "a home away from home."[5] The JCC truly advocates for wellness.

At the JCC, my friends and I mobilize for war against bad nutrition and weakening muscles, defending our bodies against the natural enemies of aging. The rigorous exercise routines can be likened at times to army boot camp or line dancing. In the locker room, we develop the deepest comradely in the fight against the true enemy of declining health and form the most loving and supportive grass-roots ecumenical relationships. As we advocate for wellness, we build up our bodies, maintaining relationships with comrades. Even during times of stress and health challenges, we are bringing a sense of Shalom to our lives through advocating for wellness.

If we wish to declare war on war itself, then we must engage in a quest for its root causes. That involves a search into the depths of the human psyche, and we cannot do this alone.[6]

Opposite page: Martha (right) in Water Aerobics Class at the York, PA, Jewish Community Center in October, 2022.

Prayer

O God,

I beseech you to empower me to declare war against the detrimental forces that afflict war on my body: improper nutrition and exercise.

Endow me with the resolve to promote my overall wellness and eradicate the adversaries of well-being in my life.

Get me moving, Lord, and ready to declare war, not only on poverty, but on my own physical, spiritual and mental poverty.

Surround me with a community that inspires me to prioritize my health through wholesome routines and self-care and may I always honor and preserve my body as a temple of Your Holy spirit!

I pray in Jesus' name.

Amen.

CHAPTER TWELVE

A Time to Embrace and a Time to Refrain from Embracing

(Ecclesiastes 5:5)

A Time to Hug

The word "embrace" in the original Hebrew means "to grasp or hold (something or someone) tightly in your arms, usually with fondness."[1] This word includes friendships, family interactions and sexual relations. The word "embrace" is also often used in scripture to describe two people greeting one another. In Genesis 29:13, for example, Laban enthusiastically welcomes his nephew Jacob, as an "embrace"; later, in Genesis 33:4, brothers Esau and Jacob have their emotional reunion as an "embrace." In the New Testament, believers are said to have regularly embraced and greeted one another with "a holy kiss" (2 Cor.13:12).

During my participation in Intervarsity Christian Fellowship while a student at Carnegie-Mellon University, I became acquainted with the practice of hugging within the context of worship. As a teenager, I had held inhibitions about hugging someone of the opposite sex. I was very shy about showing affection in such a casual way. A wise pastor instructed us one night on the beauty of hugging. After several weeks in the group, I became more comfortable with the practice. As I became more secure with my sexuality and matured, I was able to drop most inhibitions about hugging others. Later while living in other countries, I transitioned naturally into sharing the warm cultural practices of embracing.

Most of the churches that I served have had a Pennsylvania Dutch heritage. Members tended to be more formal using handshakes as a greeting and to pass the peace. With the last congregation that I pastored, St. Paul United Church of Christ in Shrewsbury, Pennsylvania, the folks warmly shared the passing of the peace often by hugging during worship—up until the outbreak of COVID in 2020.

ACTION STEP #15

Take Time to Pass the Peace

Hugs help us feel closer to others and serve to communicate when words seem inadequate. They can also help us feel good about ourselves and others. Social touch boosts serotonin and dopamine levels, and releases endorphins—the "feel good" hormones and a natural pain reliever. The hormone Oxytocin plays an important role in social bonding, slows down heart rate, and reduces both stress and anxiety levels.

Hugs can also instill a sense of familiarity and reconciliation with others, with whom we were once distant or estranged. In 1977, the student body of the Latin American Biblical Seminary in Costa Rica was divided due to political battles over the election of officers. Former friends and classmates weren't speaking with one another. I had been confronted repeatedly by fellow students who inquired about my choice of candidates. The situation

Opposite: Martha embracing Pastor Eva O'Diam at Dover UCC, Dover, PA, in September, 2023.

intensified until a special worship service was held in the chapel. The preacher ended the sermon, eloquently quoting these words from the Gospel of Matthew about reconciliation:

> So, when you are offering your gift at the altar, if you remember that your brother or sister has something against you, leave your gift there before the altar and go; first be reconciled to your brother or sister, and then come and offer your gift.
>
> (Matt. 5:23-24)

Then he offered these instructions derived from this passage: "Before we celebrate the Holy Sacrament of Communion, approach those from whom you are estranged and offer simple words of repentance and forgiveness and be reconciled before you receive this most Holy Sacrament."

For more than twenty minutes, the students mixed among each other, sharing tender sentiments of peace. Stefan, from Columbia, a candidate for president who had harshly confronted me earlier, offered first his hand and then a bear hug with the words, "I am so sorry, Martita, *paz*. In Spanish, *"paz"* means "Peace."

The reconciliation experienced during that service lasted longer than the election of officers that followed a week later. After this experience, the passing of the peace became even more meaningful in my life.

And finally, hugging can benefit our physical health. The practice of hugging has been identified as a mechanism for natural pain relief and a form of preventative medicine. One study, for example, monitored the hugging frequency of more than 400 adults. The subjects were then exposed to a common cold virus. "Huggers" were, surprisingly, less likely to get a cold. And even if they did get a cold, they had less severe symptoms.[2]

Prayer

O God,

Thank you for the warmth that comes from sharing and receiving hugs,

May we break free from the shackles of the fear of touch and closeness.

Free us of the inhibitions that prevent us from sharing such intimacy with others.

May they be outward expressions of the love we feel inside.

Let our hugs be symbols of peace and unity among us.

In Jesus' name we pray.

Amen.

A Time to Distance Socially

When the COVID pandemic struck, much of our social contact—including and *especially* embracing—was forbidden. We became keenly aware of the distance between each other. Medical experts advised us on the importance of social distancing and wearing masks. There were other constant reminders including the warnings on doors, footprint stickers on the floors of public spaces, and barriers to church pews all reminding us to distance from one another.

It was sad, going to the grocery store wearing masks and keeping a distance from each other as we pushed carts down the narrow aisles. One could not tell if others were smiling or frowning, and it was rare to hear a friendly "hello."

For many people, the thing missed most during the pandemic was being able to hug loved ones. Indeed, it wasn't until we lost our ability to hug friends and family that many realized just how important touch is to our mental health.

On the other hand, there were some positive aspects to the social distancing. From living in a family, I have learned that others need time and space to decompress. I learned this important lesson regarding the need for space on a 25th wedding anniversary cruise through the British Isles. I am a 5 a.m. riser while my husband David prefers 9 a.m. As a result, we eat breakfast at different times. With buffet food always available on the ship, it was not a problem eating anytime we wanted to do so.

Wanting to be romantic, I decided to eat a second breakfast with my husband at 9 a.m., that is, until he mentioned that my presence at his breakfast table was too much togetherness in the morning. I learned my lesson that day.

We recently celebrated our 40th wedding anniversary and we now carefully respect each other's need for space. David has his a "man cave" and I have my "she shed." We visit each other's space in the cave and shed, but we honor boundaries we have established. We have found that a necessary ingredient for peace in our marriage is allowing each other the proper social distance.

When we adopted our cat, Carrie Sierra, we were told that she was a very affectionate cat but needed periods of time to decompress. I have also observed my son, Andrew, as he matured from the cradle to adulthood needing more and more space until he eventually moved out of our home.

ACTION STEP #16:

Take Time for Social Distancing

Humans need time and space to decompress and recharge our batteries—to avoid becoming overwhelmed by external stimuli. Insufficient alone-time can lead to irritability, resentfulness, and other consequences that can cause conflict in relationships. Finding a quiet nook to read a book, having a private space to pursue a hobby, or taking a walk on one's own are all individual activities that help us feel refreshed, energized, and ready to give our best selves in our relationship.

Though large signs in stores no longer warn us to social distance, we must still be sensitive to others' needs for comfortable space and their fears of catching contagions. As we develop a natural pattern of proper distancing, we feel more comfortable facing inevitable crowds in social situations.

Prayer

O God,

Make me more aware of the proper distance needed between me and others to maintain healthy relationships.

Calm me down in crowds when anxiety causes me to pressure others in line.

Replace that anxiety with smiles and friendly conversation.

Make me considerate of others when I am feeling infectious.

Allow me to decompress in such a way that when the proper time comes, I will be ready to welcome once again the touch of my fellow human beings.

In Jesus' name I pray.

 Amen.

CHAPTER THIRTEEN

A Time to Get and a Time to Lose

(Ecclesiastes 3:6)

A Time to Get

As a teen, I went with my mother to see an off-Broadway production of *Man of La Mancha*. Since then, I have seen this show performed on film and in theaters at least ten times. The first time I saw the show, I identified with Don Quixote's impossible dream—a better life. He saw those "scorned" by society as valuable. He found worth in the prostitute, Aldonza, by calling her "Dulcinea." It has always felt like I have been on my own quest to improve the world—a quest that defies the stark realities of life. Through God, I have faith that I can make a difference.

In the story, there is a point where Don Quixote is confronted by his mortal enemy—a man called the "Knight of the Mirrors." When his nemesis insults Aldonza, Quixote challenges him to combat. Swinging huge, mirrored shields, the knight and his attendants blind Quixote with a glare. The knight taunts Quixote and forces him to see himself as the world sees him: a fool and a madman. Quixote collapses, weeping.

The Knight of the Mirrors removes his helmet and discloses that he is really Dr. Carrasco, who has a plan to cure Don Quixote's madness. But this is not the end of the story. Aldonza reminds Quixote of his impossible dream and stirs him to sing the final chorus: "To live with your heart striving upward, To a far unattainable sky."

Martha imitating Don Quixote de La Mancha in Central Park, New York City.

Such bold words inspire and motivate me. There are occasions when I have been impatient listening to stark realists. I prefer more optimistic positions, especially when extended discussions leave little time to discuss action. I tend to err on the side of speed in my eagerness to find immediate solutions, instead of engaging in long, rhetorical debates.

The Apostle Paul had a similar optimistic outlook, even though he was imprisoned and martyred for his faith. He wrote to the Philippians from prison to encourage them to continue to strive upward:

Finally, brothers and sisters, whatever is true, whatever is honorable, whatever is just, whatever is pure, whatever is pleasing, whatever is commendable, if there is any excellence and if there is anything worthy of praise, think about these things.

As for the things that you have learned and received and heard and noticed in me, do them, and the God of peace will be with you (Philippians 4:8-9).

Paul is encouraging the Philippians to search. He held before them a vision to discover the admirable and pure and commendable with quixotic vigor that is embodied in my quest for Shalom.

ACTION STEP #17

Take Time to Organize

Though one may risk appearing as insane as Don Quixote, there can be a sense of Shalom in reaching for the stars. Early in therapy, I learned the initial symptoms of mental illness include forgetfulness, misplacing items, losing one's organizational skills, and feeling overwhelmed. Success to reaching seemingly impossible dreams and arriving to a sense of peace is often making lists! What do you want to accomplish? Which goals are more important? Think about how you can best accomplish these goals. Are their measurable objectives that can help you achieve your goals?

Once one's goals and objectives are identified and prioritized, there are more lists, for example: to-do lists, packing lists, shopping lists, and contact lists. For me, the lists are simply documents on my computer that can easily be edited and printed each time I start to feel overwhelmed. For those more technically savvy than me, there are all sorts of apps that can encourage and simplify list-making. I celebrate each time something is crossed off a list.

Organization and planning can also help when you find forgetting details or misplacing items is generating stress. Forgetting where one put something is not only frustrating, but it can also be costly in terms of time and money—especially when an unauthorized person takes advantage of the situation or you must replace an item.

Here are some other strategies to help you remember where things have been placed:

- Designate a specific place for putting each item—a hook for hanging house keys, a specific section of the parking lot when at the grocery store.

- Make an item stand out. Use a large, colorful key ring and place bills to be paid in a red folder.

- Set up a routine for a series of activities and always do them in the same order, for example: (1) where you place your hat, (2) wallet, (3) phone, (4) keys, and

(5) coffee cup as you enter or exit your home.

- Use technology. Smart phones cameras let you quickly take a picture of the specific paint you need at the grocery store. Parking apps can capture the location of your car in a parking lot. And new locator tags use GPS to tell you where you left your wallet or mobile phone!

And when all else fails, take a breath and be kind to yourself. No one is perfect. Everyone has occasional mental lapses!

Prayer

O God,

In quiet time I come before you, just as I am, whether overwhelmed or disorganized, or calm and organized.

If I am feeling over-stressed, grant me the ability to adopt strategies that will allow me once again to take some control in my life.

When I find this impossible to do, grant me quiet moments of rest until the natural organization within me emerges and the feelings of being frightfully overwhelmed disappear.

If I am calm and organized, instill in me a sense of gratitude for the Shalom that I feel.

In these times, may I savor the high moments of knowing that everything is in its proper place.

In Jesus' name, I pray.

Amen.

A Time to Lose

With the 1960s' backdrop of hippies, Woodstock, peace rallies, and drug experimentation, I was a preacher's kid with strictly enforced moral codes. It shouldn't be surprising this caused me to have an identity crisis. I questioned every aspect of my belief system and wondered who I was. I found it difficult to find a peer group with whom I could relate in high school. It was not until college when I started attending a Catholic Mass folk service and then joined the Intervarsity Christian Fellowship that I began feeling some peace within myself.

I was a sophomore in college when I first realized I was experiencing an "identity crisis." I struggled with the issues of identity, status, and my place in society as an adult. While I wanted to make a difference in society, I gave up earlier ambitions of wanting to be rich and famous. I just wanted to blend in with the masses as an anonymous hard worker. I switched majors from vocal music to modern languages and literature. It was during this period of uncertainty when I finally answered my call to the ministry and began preparing to enter seminary.

Throughout this difficult period of introspection, I began to find solace in German poetry. Berthold Brecht became a particular favorite of mine. Brecht's poem, "A Worker Reads History" spoke to me. In it, he inquires, "Who built the seven gates of Thebes?" And he answers: "The books are filled with names of kings. / Was it the kings who hauled the craggy blocks of stone?" And he concludes: "Frederick the Great triumphed in the Seven Years War," but

> Every ten years a great man,
> Who paid the piper?

So many particulars.
So many questions.[1]

In these words, I identified with those who made their contribution as part of the anonymous masses, whose cumulative efforts shaped history.

Another identity crisis surfaced following my breakdown in Istanbul, Turkey. When we experience rapid changes in our lives, we can lose sight of who we are. Events and traumas such as moving, a job loss, and the end of a personal relationship can be quite bewildering and leave us vulnerable.

I found support after Istanbul in reading the poetry of Dietrich Bonhoeffer. Bonhoeffer was a great theologian of the 20th century who was martyred in the Tegel Concentration Camp for his part in the assassination plot of Hitler. In stanzas of his poem "Who Am I?" written while in confinement before his death, Bonhoeffer wrestles with how he is perceived by others. He concludes his identity does not rest in the opinions of others, but rather in his relationship with God:

Whoever I am, Thou knowest, O God, I am thine![2]

ACTION STEP #18

Take Time to Read Poetry and Current Events

Reading poetry can provide an outlet during periods of stress, trauma, and grief. Poetry can boost our spirits—pulling us outside our banal thoughts to develop a better perspective of the outside world. It can also help us find our place in the world and better express ourselves.

Reading about current events can help us to ground ourselves in what is happening around us. It replaces our fantasies and suspicions—connecting us with reality, what is actually happening around us. Such efforts help us surrender the past pains and grievances that haunt us while developing topics for amiable social conversations.

Prayer

O God,

We need to let go of past pain and grief which distort our perceptions of reality.

We need to look beyond such grief that blinds us from seeing what is really going on in the world today.

May we transcend the limits of self-centered introspection and discover interests beyond the mundane nature of our own thoughts.

Eliminate apathy from our minds.

Motivate us to find solace in poetry and current events as we reenter the real world.

Then re-energize us to engage with others in spirited, mutually beneficial conversations about these verses and events.

We pray in Jesus' name.

Amen.

CHAPTER FOURTEEN

A Time to Keep and a Time to Cast Away

(Ecclesiastes 3:6)

A Time to Keep

The first three decades of my life, I moved from residence to residence. I had a bedroom in my parents' homes, rustic cabins, university dorms, and my own apartments. With each transition, I found it difficult, on one hand, to decide what to take with me. On the other hand, these transitions helped me to develop a healthy assessment of what I really valued most in life and should keep.

When I turned 30, my husband David and I bought the first house we considered "our" home. For the next forty years, we lived in four different parsonages and one three-bedroom apartment. Initially, we acquired necessities like eggbeaters and couches. But as the years passed, our homes became filled with assorted gadgets and treasures that we found at auctions, church bazaars, yard sales, and department stores. Our spacious accommodation in this period allowed these acquisitions.

Since both my parents and aunt were clergy, we also accumulated a vast collection of books and important papers. There have also been their clergy robes, a home communion set and the extensive genealogical records that they passed on to me. I have accepted the role as family librarian and curator of this collection in addition to the items I have gathered as a member of the clergy. Over time, I have donated many items of historical importance to the

Evangelical and Reformed Historical Society archives that are currently held as part of the Lancaster Theological Seminary Library. Unfortunately, being a curator has also meant functioning as a trash collector for multiple, meaningless copies of outdated UCC resources and illegible scribbles that were crowding what was going to be our retirement apartment. I was finally able to put the last box of trash in a dumpster just over two years before I retired.

The memories found in my family's papers have helped me better understand myself as well as my childhood when we were together as a family. At first, I was overwhelmed with the stories of my brother Richard's frequent psychotic episodes and drug overdoses, my sister's illnesses and my parents' arguments. But as I began to sort through the 2,500 slides (which were digitized by my husband David) of birthday parties, holidays, celebrations, church festivals, vacations, and mission trips, I began to recall the much more positive aspects of my personal history. The pictorial history comforted me, and I gained a more balanced picture of the past.

ACTION STEP #19

Take Time to Curate Your Possessions

As tedious as the process is, curating one's possessions has therapeutic value for those with a mental health challenge. The sheer quantity of what we have accumulated can seem overwhelming at first. But by pacing oneself, the process can relieve the burden of storing and caring for these materials. It can soothe the soul.

The electronic storage and organization of documents can be particularly helpful as it eliminates the need for physical space to move and store boxes of papers. It also makes it possible to quickly find items when they are needed. When we have low moments, revisiting curated possessions can also help us return to a state of well-being.

Prayer

O God,

Inspire us to engage in the sometimes-tedious process of sorting through old photos, memorabilia, and files, so that we might discover truer, more accurate images of our past.

Help us to discern what to keep and what to discard as we consider the relics of the past, so that we save those items which will be of most value to our descendants.

And in doing so, aid us to curate the most helpful resources to be available in our times of distress.

May we also draw upon them as these resources as assets for sharing during occasions of celebration and family gatherings.

We pray in Jesus' name.

Amen.

A Time to Cast Away

My father-in law, Homer Boyer, lived 88 years before his death in 2001. Each time I announced I was moving to a new church, he would proclaim that I had "itchy feet." He and his wife, Mildred, and their four children lived in a three-bedroom home that he had built on land his family had lived on for centuries in Columbiana, Ohio. Construction of that house started with one room and additions were made as his family grew. His desire was to stay put, and to stay in one place.

When it was time to cast away something, he did it on his own property. The outhouse was eventually replaced by the family's septic tank. Household and other trash was burned in the yard. Old farm equipment was hauled into the woods behind the fields.

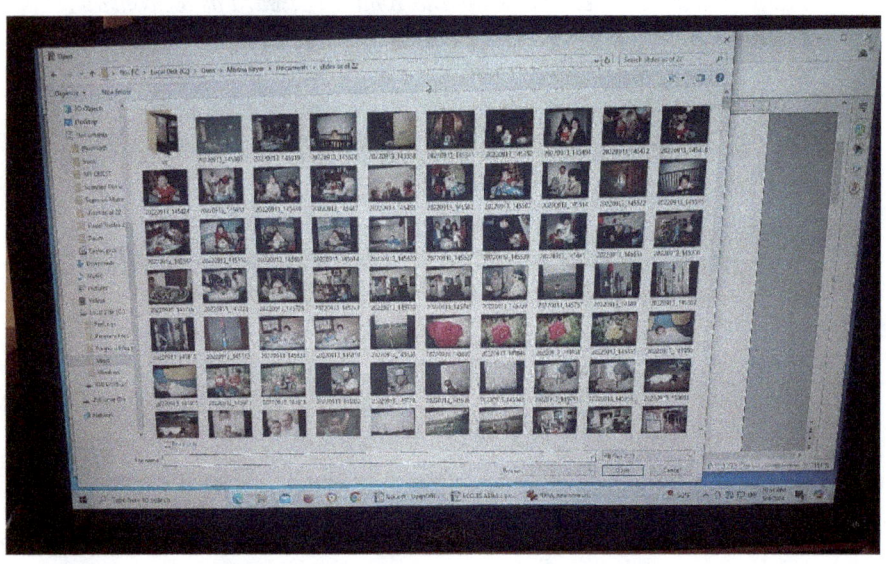

Curating 2,500 slides of Butkofsky/McConnell/Boyer Family History.

In 2024, our household trash is sorted into recyclable and non-recyclable items, picked up by trucks, and then transported to recycling centers, landfills, and incinerators. During this process, our focus was upon both cleaning up our home and protecting our environment.

Just as we need to clean up our environment, we need to clean up our lives. The Bible tells us that to love God with all one's heart, soul, mind, and strength (Mark 12:20). Sometimes, toxic relationships, addictions, and unhealthy habits prevent us from engaging on roads to recovery. To cope and make progress, we need to cast away some of our old patterns which impede our recovery. While being plagued with mental health issues, we may feel stuck, powerless, and trapped in a building without an exit. Yet no one knows us better than ourselves, so we need to develop our own action steps for particular moods during times of remission to aid in recovery and when symptoms return.

ACTION STEP #20

Take Time to Develop and Share a Plan for Self-Therapy

Mary Ellen Copeland, in an article on helpful tools for recovery, outlines a self-help strategy that she developed called the Wellness Recovery Action Plan, abbreviated as WRAP. The Plan is a structured program for people recovering from mental health conditions.[1]

To develop a Wellness Recovery Action Plan, she proposed, one must first observe one's own feelings when certain situations trigger a mental health challenge. Then one should record a list of wellness tools that can help you get and stay well during these challenges. For example, listening to music when sad, anxious, or angry; taking a walk when angry; or calling a friend when experiencing loneliness. Whether employing Copeland's strategy—she proposes 28 action steps—preparing your own self-therapy plan to avert a crisis can be life-changing. You can also advocate or help create a plan with a family member.

Do not wait to develop a plan until you are experiencing a mental health crisis. Prepare ahead of time and share it with close friends and family so they can utilize it during your most vulnerable times. They can also give you suggestions, encouragement, and feedback, especially when a crisis prevents you from taking the initiative on your own.

Be uplifted by this plan of action that dissipates your feeling of being cast away like trash. Be empowered by this process that "recycles" your depressive moods into more positive ones.

Prayer

O God,

Sometimes I feel walled-in by mental health challenges.

No one knows me better than You and me.

Help me to take responsibility for my own recovery and the steps I need to take to become well again.

Assist me in recalling the strategies that have been effective for me in managing my emotions during times of anger, frustration, despair or depression.

Use these moments of solitude to reflect upon my emotions and take the necessary actions to restore me to sanity and then....

Empower me to develop a plan for self-therapy, so that I might gain some semblance of control over my challenges.

Grant me the ability to entrust this plan with a close confidant-- family member or close friend-- that they may remind me of it in the event that I am incapacitated or am unable to recall it myself.

"Recycle" my spirit through these trusted relationships, that my self-therapy might be preventative and rejuvenating.

In Jesus' name I pray,

    Amen.

CHAPTER FIFTEEN

A Time to Rend and a Time to Sew

(Ecclesiastes 3:7)

In the Bible, rending one's clothing is a symbol of one's sorrow and vulnerability. In Genesis 37:34, Jacob grieves the loss of his son Joseph by ripping his garments. In Numbers 14, Caleb and Joshua, leaders of the exodus from Egypt, tear their clothing not out of mourning but because their people are complaining about the leadership and threatening a rebellion.

While in Lancaster in 1981 and recovering from my mental health crisis, I did not rend my clothes, but I did discover the importance of letting oneself be vulnerable. My dismay over a weight gain led me to the 12-step program Overeaters Anonymous (OA) based on similar principles in Alcoholics Anonymous. I looked to meetings of OA for support dealing with both weight management and spiritual renewal.

I worked through the entire program. Part of the process was inventorying my life and looking back on my childhood shortcomings and anxieties about mental illness. The fifth step in the program is "to admit to God, ourselves and another human being the exact nature of our wrongs."

My sponsor and I met weekly to review my personal life—the regrets and problems. We concluded by placing this inventory in her fireplace to extinguish the circumstances that I regretted. What a relief burning what had been revealed! OA taught me that we cannot carry such heavy burdens alone without admitting them to another human being and God.

ACTION STEP #21

Take Time to Be Vulnerable

Confessing things we regret—things we have done, things we ought to have done, and things others have done to us that are causing us pain—within a support network can provide both spiritual and physical healing. As we share our regrets with other human beings, we will receive God's comfort. There is also a humility experienced when we talk about our personal problems with others facing similar challenges. It also reduces feelings of shame and fear.

Within the process of sharing our true selves, we receive a new form of connection with others who then may also share their darkest moments with us. Consequently, we develop a deeper relationship with those people. When we are not vulnerable, we may appear to be secretive and unattractive, but as we display more vulnerability, we have the potential of developing greater intimacy.

As we display a well-balanced vulnerability in our relationships, we become more receptive to giving and receiving comfort in social settings. Walls of distrust and suspicion can break down between us. This was true on March 28, 1979, in West Germany while I was on a confirmation retreat. I received a telegram that reported a cooling malfunction had caused a partial nuclear meltdown of the core in Reactor 2 at Three Mile Island in Harrisburg, Pennsylvania—my hometown. As I shared my fears for the safety of my family back in the United States, the confirmation students almost immediately began to share how they experienced daily fears regarding their own safety.

These fears of nuclear incident precipitated by the Cold War were feelings that they had been previously ashamed to admit.

Prayer

O God:

Help us face how good we are and how mean we are.

Give us the courage to take an honest inventory of what has been awry in our lives, to trust someone with this list, and to place it in a cleansing fire; then extinguish the scorching flames that cause us so much grief and pain.

May our inventories be met with receptive audiences and attentive listeners. as our vulnerabilities are understood.

As we share our lives with others, may the transformation from ashes to smoke bring a sense of joyful assurance of forgiveness, comfort, and gratitude to You for providing us with such a wonderful sense of Shalom.

In Jesus' name we pray.

Amen.

A Time to Sew

I have sometimes thought of myself as a "seamstress in life" as I helped to mend other people's lives together—even as I have been mending my own life back together. In a sense, I have been what Father Henri Nouwen labels a "wounded healer." He asserts that ministry requires a deep understanding of one's own wounds if we are going to successfully speak of suffering and provide comfort to others.[1]

While living at the Lancaster Theological Seminary upon my return from Turkey, I began to function and accept my mental illness. I was able to grasp the scientific explanation given by my psychiatrist that my "sensors" had become overloaded by life; my body had reacted like it had blown a fuse. I began participating in group therapy sessions that helped me regain interest and fun in doing the simple activities of life like cooking, crafts, and conversing with others. Next, I became involved in the community life at St. Peter's United Church of Christ, across from my apartment at the seminary. The charismatic pastor there encouraged me to re-enter life by singing in the choir and co-directing their Bible School. And it was during this time that I joined Overeaters Anonymous to address my weight concerns.

Once my wounds had begun to heal, I was able to reach out in service and mutual support to family and the community. Since my father's death occurred just before I left for Turkey in 1980, my mother needed attention. Though she was not physically debilitated and was able to live independently several more decades, my father's death was the source of overwhelming grief for her and left voids that had to be filled.

Transferred to me was her need for theological debate and the intimate friendship which she had previously shared with my father. He had also provided her with financial and organizational boundaries. When he died, she became in some ways an out-of-control free spirit causing extra anxiety and grief for her children.

I began to provide Mother with the guidance that she desperately needed in establishing boundaries and administering her finances. We found peace in doing the simple things in life together like baking cookies and going out for dinner. There were tense conversations and even arguments with Mother as I took on these new responsibilities, but our changing relationship also gave me good experience in listening and forbearance as a pastor.

Martha on retreat in West Berlin, Germany, in February, 1979.

ACTION STEP #22

Take Time to Reconstruct

The most difficult part of getting back to a normal life after a breakdown is assessing and resuming a new and improved schedule. When a contributing factor to the cause of the breakdown was an over-stressed schedule, then much consideration must be given to resetting priorities and cutting out excessive activities. Review your calendar and give priority to regular doctor, clergy, and therapist appointments. Allow extra time in your schedule for unexpected interruptions—especially before appointments—so you are able to minimize potential anxiety and plan your questions.

Add simple social activities with others like baking, attending the theater, and going out to dinner to the new schedule. Then count the number of activities that you have scheduled in one day. At first, one major social activity every day should suffice, allowing you the time for the unexpected; more activities that may be added later after you have passed the initial stress of adjusting to the new routine.

Re-establish normal times to go to bed and get up in the morning. Also commit yourself to regular mealtime and medication schedules. Monitor the impact of your time schedules on how well you are feeling. Be patient as you get into the groove of your new schedule. Soon it will become a comfortable routine.

Rekindle relationships with family and friends whom you may have neglected. Offer an apology and simple explanation of your recent absence. Inquire about their well-being since you saw them last and catch up on the events that have transpired in their lives. Be mindful of making your dialogues balanced and not simply a one-sided description of your condition. Listen attentively to the suggestions that others make on how your relationships may be supportive as you return to normalcy.

Prayer

O God,

When we feel ripped apart and in need of mending, sew the raw edges of our lives back together.

Guide us as we empty and refill our calendar with less busyness and more simplicity.

Allow us to rediscover the simple joys in the pleasures of life: preparing food together, taking hikes, attending the theater or concerts, and shopping with friends, as well attending to the necessities of medical appointments and work obligations.

Lead us not into the temptation of overcrowding the calendar again, but rather guide us towards a well-balanced schedule of work and play, social and personal activities.

Help us to establish a new pattern that minimizes anxiety as we re-establish routines and relationships that will enrich our life together.

In Jesus' name we pray.

Amen.

A Family of Preachers: Rev. Dr. Edward O. Butkofsky; Rev. Beatrice Weaver and Frank McConnell, music minister, (just behind the table); Martha as child (right) th Rev. Mary Alice Butkofsky (behind her).

CHAPTER SIXTEEN

A Time to Keep Silent and a Time to Speak

(Ecclesiastes 3:7)

A Time to Keep Silent

You have heard it said, "Speaking is silver, but silence is golden." Growing up in a family of preachers, silence was a rare commodity. It felt like everywhere we went—church, conferences, and even at home—my parents were always talking or preaching, Often, my siblings and I returned home from late night church conferences with our parents in our pajamas. While we tried to drift to sleep in the back seat, my parents were up front talking. If we interrupted them, I never feared being punished by paddling but there was a strong possibility that there would be a long rhetorical admonition. It seemed they were almost always talking. However, they did display "golden" silence in their roles as pastors. I learned from observing my parents and other pastors there is a time to keep silent.

While serving as a pastor of Christ Church United Church of Christ in Norristown, Pennsylvania, in 1995 I visited a church member in the psychiatric ward of the hospital. She was a prominent member who had been diagnosed with delusions and depression. Lying in bed with her back toward me, she only turned her head to greet me with a soft, "Hello." I responded, "How are things going?" Then I stood in silence for several minutes before she began to describe the pressure at work and her shame of having a breakdown. Her body language displayed embarrassment as she began to talk freely about what she had experienced among friends and coworkers. Though my thoughts were drawn to my own personal struggles with mental health illness since 1980, I refrained from speaking and responded with empathetic, silent gestures. She slowly turned toward me, sat up, and began to share more freely of the pressures at work. I never found the right moment to tell her of my own breakdown in Istanbul. This was a time to focus on the patient and to keep silent, so that she had the opportunity to air her feelings.

As pastors, we most often enter hospital rooms with a simple, "Hello, how are things going?" followed by silence at least until we get a response from the patients on how they are doing. Then, by listening, we follow the cues from patients. By silently observing their body languages, we can ascertain when it is the proper time to speak.

ACTION STEP #21

Take Time to Be Silent

Following a traumatic mental episode can be a rawness of freshly-exposed feelings. It is easy to become preoccupied with the details of the episode and become excessively introspective. As life continues around us and we are trying to move forward, we need to consider carefully with whom and when to share our deepest thoughts:

Who can we trust with our traumatic stories?

In what situations is it appropriate to expose the details?

How can we best blend in with normal social circles?

Sharing at the wrong time with the wrong people can make one vulnerable to ridicule and condemnation. At the same time, having a trusted community can provide support and relief. We must find the proper balance between being silent and speaking up about mental health challenges in ourselves and in others

Prayer

O God,

Sometimes we simply say too much when fewer words could suffice.

Forgive us of our verbosity that discolors the pure gems that will shine forth the wisdom of God's Spirit.

In Jesus' name we pray.

Amen.

A Time to Speak

Historically, the treatment of those with mental illness involved patients in locked rooms or placed in mental health institutions for life. In a worst-case scenario, some persons were deemed witches and burned at the stake! Our culture is full of television shows and movies with mentally ill characters exhibiting socially unacceptable behaviors as persons to be feared. The stigma of mental illness is deeply ingrained in our society and those who are mentally ill have difficulty speaking about their conditions. When I learned who I could trust with my story and began to share it, I found loving support.

In the years that my family dealt with our mental health issues, I believed it was a sign of strength to hide the anguish and other emotions I was feeling. I quietly suffered the indignity and ostracism of people openly gossiping and joking about the residents of the state psychiatric hospital in Harrisburg, Pennsylvania, just a few miles from our home. Hearing their ridicule, I was privately grieving and feeling very alone. I was trying to deny what was inextricably bound to a family that had mental health issues.

I had to muster a great deal of courage when I told my future husband about my mental health issues. David listened intently then responded quickly describing his own health issues. It brought me immediate peace to find such loving acceptance and reciprocity. Since that incident over forty years ago, I have found myself in the position of sharing my diagnosis with others in a variety of personal conversations. I have often been shocked and relieved by the loving acceptance with which so many have responded. Their reaction has not been alarm or prejudice; more often than not, they shared their own mental health experiences or those of family and friends.

As I was preparing to retire last year, I began to open myself to others about my "failure" in Istanbul, Turkey. I was ready to be true to my vow to deal with my breakdown in Istanbul. I started to feel a sense of relief when I started to talk and write about what I had experienced. The talking itself was therapeutic as I practiced articulating my story and pieced together the memories of 40 years ago. Slowly, my fears of being ostracized for my medical condition were disappearing. For the first time in all those years, I had the courage to openly admit the details of what happened to me and to confront my psychiatrist for an accurate diagnosis.

On August 11, 2023, after years of misdiagnosis, I was finally told that I had schizophrenia. The identification of my condition and the steps I have taken to achieve Shalom have finally brought me to a point where I am now comfortable sharing with others my mental health challenge and what I am doing to cope with it. It also gave me the courage to more fully research what this horrible "S-word" condition is.

The most helpful explanation I have found is published in the Cleveland Clinic:

> Some symptoms of schizophrenia can possibly be caused by having too much dopamine in certain areas of your brain—delusions and hallucinations. Other symptoms are possibly caused by not having enough dopamine in another part of your brain—lack of motivation.... Dopamine is a type of neurotransmitter and hormone that plays a role in many important body functions, including movement, memory and pleasurable reward and motivation. High or low levels of dopamine are associated with several mental health and neurological diseases.... Dopamine antagonists are used to treat schizophrenia, bipolar disorder, nausea and vomiting.
>
> ....
>
> If you have the right balance of dopamine, you might feel happy, motivated, alert and focused. Conversely, with a low dopamine level, you might feel tired, unmotivated, unhappy and experience memory loss, mood swings, sleep problems, concentration problems, and a low sex drive.[1]

I am no longer ashamed to admit that I have regular counseling and take medications to stabilize the chemical imbalance caused by the dopamine level in my brain.

ACTION STEP #22

Take Time to Speak Your Truth

When we experience the challenges of mental health, we face the same five stages of grief which Elisabeth Kübler-Ross, a Swiss-American psychiatrist, famously identified in her 1969 book, *On Death and Dying*. Those stages are *denial, anger, bargaining, depression,* and *acceptance*. Only when we reach acceptance are we emboldened to speak out in a positive way against the stigma of suffering from mental illness.[2]

Ascending to the level of self-acceptance is a long and challenging journey—particularly for those who have experienced the amnesia and mindless out-of-control behavior associated with some mental illnesses. Accepting any mental illness means facing realities over which we have absolutely no control. It is taking medications that will restore the balance in our body chemistry while paying attention to possible undesirable side effects. There is also a need for spiritual acceptance—forgiveness for any shame we feel from the behaviors that accompany our illness.

Thankfully, social attitudes towards mental health are changing in the United States. While some stigma remains, an overwhelming majority of adults now harbor mostly positive views about mental health. Most report that having a mental health disorder is nothing to be ashamed and that those with mental health disorders can get better.

Credit for this change in opinion must largely be given to the doctors and researchers who have identified new medications and other forms of treatment for those suffering from a mental illness. But substantial credit must also be given to individuals who have publicly advocated the need to eliminate the stigmas and those who have acknowledged their personal mental health challenges.

First Lady Rosalynn Carter tirelessly advocated for people living with mental illness. Catherine Marie Shetler, a registered nurse and former wife of Penn Northeast Conference Minister, Rev. Dr. John C. Shetler, advocated with the National Alliance for Mental Illness (NAMI) to help destroy the stigmas associated with mental illness within the United Church of Christ. These two women, Rosalynn Carter and Catherine Marie Shetler, along with the resources of NAMI, paved the way for those of us newly motivated to muster our forces and declare war on this worst of enemies: mental illness.

Mike Wallace is an example of a public figure who found the courage to share his personal experience with depression and become a highly visible advocate for those similarly afflicted. An award-winning reporter for the CBS television news magazine, *60 Minutes,* Wallace had his first major bout of depression triggered in 1984, after US Army General William C. Westmoreland sued him and several others for libel for a television documentary on the Vietnam War. Wallace was lauded by peers and mental health experts alike for publicly acknowledging his mental illness.

When we begin to accept our own diagnoses and mental health challenges as a normal part of life, we are more comfortable about sharing them. Knowing when the appropriate time to share this information then becomes more natural.

And then: we learn how to speak up for those who cannot!

Prayer

O God,

Help us to accept the things we cannot change about our own physical, spiritual, and mental health.

Help us to overcome our self-prejudices that keep us from having a positive attitude towards life.

Inspire us with the role models of those who have pioneered the way for us to move forward with our advocacy of mental health issues.

Thank you for the courage of their witnesses and their victory over the long-held stigmas against mental illness, from which we have all benefited.

May we also boldly speak out in ways that allow others to accept our own gifts that exist despite our limitations.

In Jesus' name we pray.

Amen.

CHAPTER SEVENTEEN

A Time to Love and a Time to Hate

(Ecclesiastes 3:8)

A Time to Love

What better way to focus on serving others than in participating in a work camp? Throughout my ministry, I found a deep sense of worth and peace participating in numerous work camps. In Auschwitz, I helped rake leaves. I have tended animals and crops in three Heifer International Work Camps and painted walls in local church camps. There is also the time I helped renovate homes of hurricane victims in Mississippi with a Samaritan's Purse project. Not only does this benevolent outreach provide gratification through sweat equity in a worthwhile project, but it also yields an outpouring of gratitude from those whose lives have been touched by the outreach.

At the closing celebrations for each camp, the workers and the projects' recipients gave heart-warming testimonies of how the love of God had been demonstrated to them through the selfless service of those who donated time and effort. Participating in work camps gives one a warm feeling that individual efforts can make a difference.

Participating in work camps serving others is also a way in which I take my mind off myself—focusing on serving and loving others. It always gives me a sense of Shalom.

ACTION STEP #25

Take Time to Serve Others and Show You Care

Dealing with a mental illness can wear us out. There is a tendency to become introspective and self-centered, even feeling victimized. Key to finding peace within is exploring what we can do for others. Consider, for example, Helen Keller or others who overcame great odds and focused their energy on serving others. Muster the gifts you have been given to reach out to others in love.

There are extensive lists in on-line articles of how to serve others. I will only summarize the best three that I have found on-line and provide you with their website addresses.

- "100 Ways to Serve Others": This list provides the 100 practical ways one can serve others.

    https://busylivingpretty.wordpress.com/2010/02/14/100-ways-to-serve-others/

- "10 Ways to Serve Someone Today" by Anna Collin" provides ten practical ways one can serve someone today, based upon Biblical principles.

    https://newspring.cc/articles/10-easy-ways-to-serve-someone-today

- "Fast and Powerful Ways You Can Serve Others" by Andrew Thomas shares seven ways to find a genuine sense of fulfillment and purpose.

    https://www.inc.com/andrew-thomas/7-ways-to-serve-others-despite-your-busy-schedule.html

Take time to serve others and show you care by checking out these websites for suggestions how you can make a difference in the lives of others.

As you engage in some of these ways of serving others, may you find peace within.

Prayer

O God,

Open our eyes to see beyond the jagged walls of pain that trap us inside ourselves and isolate us from others.

Bring authentic love into our lives; let love and care flow naturally.

Free us from feeling we must act in love out of obligation.

Instead saturate us with love that permeates every part of our bodies and then overflows authentically in our surrounding community—especially in those so much in need of divinely-inspired love.

May our words of love inspire deeds of love, that will propel us forward on our quests for Shalom.

We pray in Jesus' name.

Amen.

Martha's final communion service at St. Paul United Church of Christ in Shrewsbury: Pastor Laura Bair (to left) and Conference Minister Rev. Dr. Carrie Call.

A Time to Hate

Though in later years, my brother Richard and I were best buddies, it is hard for me to admit that I had hateful feelings toward him when we were children. I hated the attention he got as the youngest child. I may not have realized it at the time, but there were probably ill feelings because he got special treatment as my parents' long-awaited male child.

Richard and I had a classic sibling rivalry as we competed for the attention of our parents and found ways to annoy each other. One Halloween, Richard dressed up as a red devil. On occasions over the next year when I was particularly irritated by the attention he was getting from my parents or something he was doing, I would sit down at the piano and play a mocking jingle, "Richard is a devil." There reached a point when all I needed to do was to hit the first six notes of the jingle on the piano and I would get an immediate shrieking rise from him. No matter where he was in the house, he could hear my hateful tune.

Looking back, I realize I never really hated Richard, I only hated his actions and the circumstances of our lives.

ACTION STEP #26

Take Time to Identify Triggers

No matter the state of one's mental health, we all have triggers: words, actions, circumstances, and other stimuli that elicit reactions. What triggers a reaction in you? By identifying our triggers, we can reflect upon why we react as we do and seek out ways to avoid them. In those situations where we can't avoid them, how can we cope with them?

I have a list of things that trigger me. Among those on my list are:

1. Being late.

2. Financial insecurity.

3. Feelings of being overwhelmed.

4. Being surrounded by conflict.

5. Not knowing what will happen in the future and, hence, not being prepared.

6. Being alone.

7. Not understanding as well as not being understood.

In my case, all of my triggers center around the inability to control events. I hate feeling so powerless.

Triggers are different for everyone; as such, the strategies for coping with them also differ.

To provide an example of how I try to liberate myself from the anxiety created by my triggers, here are the three top strategies I employ:

STIMULI	STRATEGY
1. Lateness	Always plan to arrive 10 minutes early.
2. Financial insecurity	Create a detailed budget.
3. Overwhelming feelings	Make task lists and prioritize.

Prayer

O God,

Sometimes we feel trapped within ourselves by the triggers that seem to control us. We sometimes vehemently hate our mental illness and deny our struggle exists.

As we are walled-in by heavy emotional weights of hate within us and around us that prevent us from acting, help us to find ways to rise above the fears that debilitate us.

May the energy of triggers which is so overpowering be harnessed instead into doing some good work in the world.

May we find new strategies that will allow us to transform our hate into the love and tranquility of self-improvement.

May we be aware of the triggers of hate and be empowered to overcome them with new strategies.

We pray in Jesus' name.

Amen.

Mother (left) protesting the War in Washington, DC.

CHAPTER EIGHTEEN

A Time for War and a Time for Peace

(Ecclesiastes 3:8)

War is insane, and yet, in Ecclesiastes, Solomon suggests there is a time for it. In the face of brute force, standing up for oneself may be necessary, but we should not do so without considering the potential consequences.

Living near the bomb-damaged buildings that remained in Germany thirty years after World War II; listening to the testimonies of concentration camp survivors and war veterans; and then experiencing a military coup in Istanbul has made the horrors of war very real for me. Yet nothing had a greater impact than the three-week trip I took to Poland in the Spring of 1980 to work with the Youth from the German-speaking Dietrich Bonhoeffer Parish Church in West Berlin.

Living in the former SS Barracks in Auschwitz for ten days, I walked through rows and rows of gas showers and crematoriums built by Adolph Hitler and the Nazis. I spoke with survivors who endured extreme forms of torture and humiliation in the death camps. One former prisoner spoke to us of his job shoveling out the cremated human remains. I saw prosthesis from the physically challenged stored as trophies and skin tattoos shaved from the arms of prisoners fashioned into pocketbooks.

One evening we interviewed a man who had been incarcerated in Auschwitz for several years. After he was freed, he chose to live in a house less than a mile from the camp. He painted and visited youth groups who toured the camp. Seeing the lovely paintings decorating the walls of his small home. I asked him why he painted such beautiful pictures of nature. "Why not paint pictures of the horrors that he saw—anguished human beings and dead bodies?"

He answered quickly, "I painted such pictures then and now because these beautiful objects of creation are what inspired me and helped me to endure the trauma that I experienced while living during the war. They help me deal with the horror even now."

This man, like others who have experienced the worst trauma, found inspiration in walking among and painting beautiful scenes of flowers, birds, and trees that grow even on the outskirts of a horrible death camp. Such scenery provides hope in a God who creates beauty in the very spots that were so stained by the blood of war and polluted by the smell of burning flesh.

ACTION STEP #27

Take Time to Create Beauty

When faced with mental illness, regular encounters with beauty can help us overcome suffering. Better yet, find a way to add beauty to the world: paint beautiful scenes of nature, play a musical instrument, take photos of people doing good deeds, write poetry, sew a colorful quilt. In other words, find and use one of your God-given talents to add beauty to your environment and that of others. These efforts can be a powerful tool for overcoming the trauma of a mental illness.

Occupying our time by creating beauty not only rids our minds of negative thoughts but also gives us the self-satisfaction of creating something that might inspire others. Collaborating with others in the creation of such beauty has a bonus of bringing constructive change to our life together. Creating beauty is the penultimate action step on my quest for Shalom–bringing peace to our communities and world.

Prayer

O God,

When our spirits feel crushed and it seems we have lost touch with life as it was meant to be, reconnect us with the beauty in our world so we may regain a clear view of life as it was intended.

Creator God, Your creation exudes beauty and goodness from its inception. As stewards of the earth, guide us in crafting objects that reflect your glory and bring joy to the senses.

Awaken in us the desire to cultivate that which is beautiful: gardens and landscapes, paintings and sculptures, quilts and afghans, and all sorts of graphics and innovative projects.

Through the adoption of these innovative practices, might we bring life back to the way it was intended to be.

We pray in Jesus' name.

Amen.

A Time for Peace

It is significant that Solomon ends his series of couplets in Ecclesiastes with a "Time for Peace." In my ongoing search for Shalom, I aspire for mental, physical, and spiritual wellness. I have also sought tranquility with myself, God, and others.

I have found what I refer to as "Shalom communities" are fundamental to finding this peace. My husband and I reside in such a community in Powder Mill Apartments in York, Pennsylvania. We reside in a residence under the tall oaks of a campus that is dedicated to enhancing community spirit among its residents. The design of the apartment complex, the Community Center, a pool and specially planned activities provides an exceptionally fine community life with neighbors of all ages.

The church is also an important shalom community for me. Paul described the early church as the Body of Christ, containing many members like a human body with every part needed for proper functioning. No one can rightfully exclude another from that body for it to function well. I find Shalom functioning in the church, knowing that no one can be excluded. As a pastor for 45 years, I have seen the church evolve to welcome people with diverse backgrounds and challenges. The United Church of Christ shows compassion and welcomes those who suffer from mental illness.

ACTION STEP #28

Take Time for Conciliatory Prayer

The United Church of Christ Statement of Faith affirms that "God was in Christ reconciling the world unto himself."[1] Seek reconciliation with God and others through the power of prayer. Stop praying as I did, petitioning, "Lord help me to forget and deny what ever happened during these mental breaks in my life." Instead, pray:

Martha with water aerobics instructor Debbie McLaughlin at the Powder Mill Pool in June, 2024.

> *O God,*
>
> *If this is a part of who I am, please help me to understand and deal with it so that I might live a normal life and help others with similar challenges be at peace with their diagnosis.*
>
> *Amen.*

Approach God in prayer and look for answers to those prayers.

My prayer—*"Lord help me to forget and deny what ever happened during these mental breaks in my life"*—was answered, not with immediate insights into my condition on how I might help others, but with an unanticipated full-blown relapse. In this case, it came during the writing this book, near Easter of 2023. Could this relapse have been an answer to my prayer? During my five-day hospital rehabilitation, I received intensive therapy and developed new insights into my condition. In the months since this most recent episode, I have accepted my psychiatrist's diagnosis and treatment plan as one that will help me live a long and healthy life—spiritually, physically, and mentally.

Once again, I pray that you be at peace with your diagnosis. Be supported by the "Shalom communities" where you live and where you worship. Let go of your anger at God for your disease and take time for daily conciliatory prayer, thanking God for the opportunities to serve God that only exist because of your diagnosis. Celebrate your resilience and reconciliation with God in Shalom communities!

Prayer

O God,

Be here for us on our ongoing quest for Shalom.

We long to love unconditionally and be ambassadors of peace in a world torn apart by conflict. Fill our hearts with kindness and guide us on the path to sublime tranquility that defies human understanding.

Preserve the love relationship with us, neither too cold nor too hot, and give us the resilience and fortitude to keep it up. Create pure hearts in us and reconcile us to You and others, bringing back the joy of genuine peace.

Create a Shalom-centered community on earth, where individuals can find inner peace and live in unity with each other.

We pray in Jesus' name.

Amen.

CONCLUSION

I began writing this book not knowing how it would end but hoping it would draw me a little closer in my quest for Shalom. I did not realize how difficult it would be to write about such painful times in my life, nor did I anticipate the closure that it has brought as I have come to ultimately accept the traumas as part of my life. In addition to providing this book as a resource on mental health for others, it is my hope that if faced with a relapse, I might read and find help in these same resources for recovery.

While writing, I was challenged by my pastor to answer the following question: "How can a pastor with mental health challenges draw strength from the other two areas of the Trinity: body and spirit?" The three parts of our bodies: physical, spiritual, and mental are so integrally connected that treating any one of these three parts positively affects the other two. Taking hikes and exercising are often recommended to relieve emotional distress. The rhythmic movement in African American churches produces a kind of euphoric sense of well-being among the worshipers. Removing a splinter from a foot will not only alleviate the pain but relieve the emotional upset and heal the spirit. Similarly, mental or spiritual treatments can enhance our physical health. In like manner, as we receive treatment for our mental ailments, we may become more enthusiastic in all three aspects of wellness!

The 28 action steps outlined in this book have been chosen to encourage those of us experiencing a mental health challenge to face it pro-actively. The steps have physical, mental and spiritual components. As we engage in them, Shalom draws nearer.

Each chapter provides prayers asking for God's help in my ongoing quest for Shalom—petitioning God for peace through wellness. Praying these prayers instills in me the peace that Paul described in Philippians 4:7: "The peace of God which passes all of our understanding." Praying the Psalms also instills a sense of shalom. When King David experienced mental anguish over his adulterous affair with Bathsheba, he prayed:

> Create in me a clean heart, O God,
>   and renew a right spirit within me.
> Cast me not away from thy presence
>   and take not thy holy spirit from me.
> Restore unto me, the joy of my salvation,
>   and uphold me with a willing spirit.
> (Psalm 51:10-12)

Such prayers offer consolation to those in mental anguish. They can reconcile us not only with God but with each other and bring true peace that passes our understanding.

Throughout my quest, I have grappled with my own diagnosis and sought to explain this complex disease in medical terms easy for others to understand. Here is my conclusive explanation: Though much research remains to be done to determine how dopamine works in everyone through transmitters and hormone, Schizophrenia is a chemical imbalance in which the neurotransmitters (primarily dopamine) in the brain go haywire and cause sensory overload. The right drug match is needed to restore balance. That right drug match can vary from person to person. But this can be done rather quickly with the right medication (as in my case) or it can take longer, as each individual does not respond to the same chemicals and therapy. The drugs do not cure the condition, but in many cases make it possible to thrive in main-stream society.

In *My Quest for Shalom* I have moved from being totally secretive about my diagnosis—secretive even unto myself—towards accepting my mental illness as a part of who I am as a person. This acceptance emphatically does not place mental illness as the center stage of my identity as a person or as a pastor. I have come to understand that mental illness is no worse than any other disease. At times, it is even preferable to many others. It is rarely life threatening, though it is scary and can induce fear in others. One can lead a normal life with a satisfying family and career as I have.

Solomon wrote that "For everything there is a time and a time for every purpose under heaven." My hope is that ours is a time for medical breakthroughs for those who are mentally distraught!

More than ever, I yearn for peace in our world.

More than ever, I believe that peace in the world begins with me and every individual.

More than ever, I believe that peace begins as we engage in our own personal quests for Shalom.

A PRAYER OF HOPE

for Pastors Facing Mental Health Challenges

Here we are Lord, in response to Your call, despite our weakness and confusion!

We have been plagued by delusions and failed to control our behavior, causing embarrassment and questioning our divine mission.

However, You have empowered us to recover through medication, therapy, and supportive communities, you forgive shame and make us feel like precious Children of God once again.

Now, may we reaffirm our commitment to serving You and Your people, partnering with mental health professionals, and utilizing our understanding of schizophrenia and other mental health conditions to strive for shalom and compassion in overcoming our difficulties, just as You overcame death and rose from the pit of despair.

Having seen the worst of Hell and witnessed the Resurrected Lord rise above it, inspire us to pursue paths of triumph over despair.

With the guidance of medical professionals, therapists, and mental health advocates, help us to overcome our own struggles with schizophrenia, depression, and other mental health issues.

Provoke in us passion to empower others to embrace a life characterized by peace and wholeness.

Here we are again, Lord, in response to your call, having found hope on our on-going quests for Shalom!

Amen!

APPENDIX ONE

RESOURCES

Organizations

Jewish Community Center
https://yorkjcc.org/

National Alliance on Mental Illness (NAMI)
https://www.nami.org/

United Church of Christ Mental Health Network
https://www.mhn-ucc.org/

Wise For Mental Health:
Congregation/Synagogue/Organization Toolkits
https://www.mhn-ucc.org/congregational-toolkits/

Books

Sarah Grifith Lund, *Blessed Are the Crazy: Breaking the Silence about Mental Illness, Family, & Church* (Chalice Press).

Daniel G. Amen, *Change Your Brain, Change Your Body: Use Your Brain to Get and Keep the Body You Have Always Wanted* (Random House).

Ken Duckworth, *You Are Not Alone: the NAMI Guide for Navigating Mental Health* (Zando/NAMI National).

APPENDIX TWO[1]

A THEOLOGICAL-EDUCATIONAL EXPERIENCE IN LATIN AMERICA

Martha Helene Butkofsky

FIRST IMPRESSIONS

McDonald's, Hardee's, Kodak, Helen Curtis, the Playboy Club, Coca Cola and Pepsi--these neon signs greeted me when I arrived in Costa Rica on January 6, 1977. I felt as though I was still on the outskirts of New York City. Twelve months have passed and I now have a new understanding of Latin America. At first I thought of Costa Rica as a small Latin American country differing very little from Small Town, USA, but that impression was shattered shortly after my arrival. My New York gallop kept me out-of-step with the people on the street, but I gradually slowed down to a Latin American stroll. My *gringo* sense of time isolated me from my new friends, so I adopted *Tico* time. I was careful, even tight with money, until I met people unable to obtain the mere necessities of life. My approach to the "theology of liberation" was radically transformed through my experiences with those whose theological position is not a matter of rhetoric but an encounter with contemporary problems. Though the answers have not yet been determined fully, they will be encountered on the way with Jesus Christ.

QUESTIONS AND ANSWERS

"Not reading and speculation, but living, dying, and being condemned make a real theologian." These words of Luther, used in the thesis of José Míguez-Bonino's, *Doing Theology in a Revolutionary Situation*, pinpointed my reasons for wanting to study for a year at the Latin American Biblical Seminary in San José, Costa Rica. It was my objective to prepare for parish and world ministries, not only to obtain a solid education in Bible, theology, church history and Christian ethics, but also to become a "living, dying and condemned" theologian who refutes hypocrisy and in Pauline dedication lives the gospel and fosters God's kingdom. I could only achieve these objectives through the coupling of an intense and essential practical education with academic courses.

My experiences in Costa Rica formed an important part of my theological education and gave me the opportunity to study Christian responsibility to the oppressed from a Third World perspective. I arrived in Costa Rica with many questions and sometimes the responses to these questions raised new ones.

What is the future of missions when voices from the Third World are calling, "Moratorium," and shouting accusations of imperialistic paternalism?

Courses with Robert McAffee Brown, Roger Shinn and Letty Russell in the field of "Ecumenics" and "World Christianity" brought this question to the forefront of my thinking during my studies at Union Theological Seminary in New York. On the Council of Theological Students of the United Church Board for World Ministries and the Oikoumene Committee we wrestled with this issue. All of us had been deeply challenged and felt the impact of the "Open Letter to North American Christians."

My classmates at the seminary in San José had varied reactions to missionaries. Some had had very positive relationships with missionaries who had touched their lives in very special ways. Others had had negative experiences. Missionaries had arrived along with multinational companies and the CIA and had been suspected of close associations with the latter. Almost all of my classmates hoped that economic dependence on U.S. mission boards could be severed, yet they realized that such a break was economically impossible at the present time.

Besides the development of a critical conscience and a firm critique of present realities, what are the positive alternatives that lie before us? This was one of the pressing questions on my mind as I attended the Continental Consultation of CELEP along with pastors, representatives from boards and commissions and leaders of churches and organizations dedicated to pastoral ministries in Latin America. The participants analyzed the actual state of present programs and ministries and developed a continental strategy for theological education, youth programs, the congregation, and women. Orlando and Rose Costas were the organizers and coordinators of the conference. Because of my interest in missiology, I registered for a course in "Faith and Ideology" taught by José Míguez-Bonino, visiting professor from Buenos Aires, and Paul Leggett of the faculty of Biblical Seminary. One third of the course was a critique of the ideologies of the 19th century missionary movement, with special attention given to the identification of dualisms. My final paper for this course was entitled, "Missionary Hymns: Faith or Ideology?".

During the second semester I studied "Missiology" with Orlando Costas. I began to understand the biblical and theoretical basis of missions and felt an awareness of contemporary trends in the missionary movement. I now began to see missions, which for me had been synonymous with paternalistic imperialism, as positive and vital. "The Ecumenical Problem of Evangelization," my final paper for the course, is a crucial issue in Latin America where a variety of ecumenical forms exist though they often appear in fiery ideological confrontation--a confrontation which dissolves the unity necessary for the battling of imperialistic forces. On what level is Christian unity to be sought? Doctrinally? On the level of faith? Testimony? Praxis? Practices? The question of unity continues to preoccupy me for it is a profoundly practical one with crucial implications for the future of mission strategy. At the Latin American Biblical Seminary, where 103 students represent 40 denominations and 17 countries, what is the tie that binds? Unity was clearly not to be found in a common ecclesiastical heritage, not in doctrine nor in national allegiance. The unity of the seminary was based on its credo, "Por Cristo y América Latina" (For Christ and Latin America).

During my last few months in San José, I became increasingly aware of the great financial and personnel necessities on the mission field. So many in Latin America look to the North for economic aid. I met many needy students and people seeking financial assitance. On the other hand, these same people were eager to witness the severence of economic and consequent cultural dependence. An end to all foreign aid, however, would mean sure death to many of the evangelical institutions in Latin America. Many students would lose the opportunity to study as well.

The actual state of the mission field in Latin America raises some very serious and challenging questions for North Americans with a world consciousness. As we listen to the pleas from a wide variety of Latin Americans, both Evangelical and Catholic, to whom do we respond with economic funding? Those whose doctrines most closely support our own state of affairs and civil religion? Are the monies and priorities given to those who come to the U.S. seeking help while others in Latin America have to do without financial aid? Why do we continue to send missionaries to Latin America when so many qualified Latins could fill the positions with additional training? How do we in the parishes of the U.S. respond to the new voices of Latin America? Do we ignore them, or should we not mobilize in obedience to God's call to us in ways that will benefit both us and our brothers and sisters in the Third World?

*What is the nature of the new Latin America
Christology which has developed out of the
"theology of liberation"?*

In Gustavo Gutiérrez's course, "New Developments in the Theology of Liberation," I became aware that I am a white, middle class, female North American whose theology was being challenged by Third World theologians. In New York, Robert McAfee Brown's course on "Ecumenical Antecedents to Liberation Theology" introduced me to the political forces and ecclesiastical movements that formed the background of the theology. We studied documents of the World Council of Churches as well as the encyclicals of the Catholic Church and focused particularly on the recent challenges from the Third World: Medellín and Chile.

My interest increased in understanding the irreconciliable differences between North American and Latin American theology. To wrestle with these issues, I elected three courses--"Theological Methodology," an "Interdepartmental Seminar," and "Christology." In the study of "Theological Methodology" taught by Professor José Míguez-Bonino, we dealt with the epistomological, the hermeneutical, the synthetical and the dialectical aspects of both traditional and Latin American methodology. Our final project was to define the theological methodology of a contemporary theologian. My paper defined the "Hermeneutics of José Míguez-Bonino." In the "Interdepartmental Seminar," professors and students joined in an interdisciplinary debate focusing around the theme of human liberation. In "Christology," I learned the newest developments in the theology of liberation. Is there a christological gap in Latin American theology? Works of Leonardo Boff and João Sobrino had come as the first systematic responses to this gap. We studied articles from a newly published book edited by José Míguez-Bonino, *Jesús: Ni Vencido, ni Monarca Celestial*. The new Latin American Christology is a pastoral and critical theology which attempts to encounter the biblical Christ, the Christ of the Beatitudes, by unmasking an imperialistic, powerless, abstract Christ.

In Victorio Araya's course on *Latin American Theology*, I learned that the "theology of liberation" is one among many battling Latin American theologies but still a very dominant theological force.

Latin American Christology is a critical and contextualized theology which attempts to reread the Bible and ecclesiastical history, particularly the Councils of Calcedonia and Nicea, with the new Latin American optics. It is not done in "towers of marble" but in the midst of contemporary cultural realities. It does not involve the memorization

of formulas or the deduction of equations, but is an analysis of the
actual images of Christ manifest within culture and its political relations with the coming of the kingdom. As I walked through the
cathedrals of Latin America, I was struck by the elegant, Spanish imperial statues of Christ alongside of the statues depicting the suffering
Christ. Do people who daily worship an imperial Christ really encounter the biblical Christ? Do people who meditate morbidly upon the sufferings of Christ day after day know the Christ of the Beatitudes?

*How has the theology of liberation manifested
itself within the local churches of Latin
America, and what effect has it had on
biblical hermeneutics?*

Through my studies at the Latin American Biblical Seminary, I
learned that the question could have been better articulated. The
theology of liberation is more of a reflection of reality than a statement of dogmatic truths. A better phrasing of the question would be:
How do Latin American parishes "do theology"? I found answers to this
question in two of the churches I attended in San José. The Church of
Zapote, pastored by seminary professor Osvaldo Mottesi, holds a charismatic service in which the congregation and the pastor fully participate.
The pastoral prayer is not one that the pastor memorized the night before. It develops out of a conversation with the pastor and the congregation about their social and personal needs and those of the world.
In a prayer of thanksgiving the people give thanks to God spontaneously,
yet spontaneity is balanced with order in the services. Neither "the
spiritual" nor "the social" characterizes the service, but a real
commitment to Christ inseparably linked to social responsibility. During the week the congregation meets in groups for Bible study.

At the "Church of the Way" in a slum called Chapulines, Orlando
Espinoza, a seminrian from Colombia, is the minister. I worked as one
of his assistants in charge of Bible study and preaching on Tuesday
nights. "Doing theology" for these people meant praying that the government would provide houses for them this year--or at least indoor
plumbing or electricity. They established committees and attended city
council meetings to plead for their rights. Today the Chapulines congregation is rejoicing in the good news that the government has promised
them houses in the Spring. For them it is the answer to many prayers.

In contrast, people living in Nicaragua under similar conditions
have a more difficult time. According to reports from Nicaraguan

refugees, "doing theology" in Nicaragua means political condemnation because it opposes the oppression of Somoza. Ernesto Cardenal, a leader in the religious community of Solentiname, Nicaragua, describes faith in this way.

> Faith in the New Testament consists in believing that Christ is the Messiah, the Liberator who came to change the world. Faith consists of change--the Kingdom of a new and just society. It's not important to have faith in Christ as the Son of God or God. It is important to believe in Him, the Messiah, the Liberator.

To discover the new biblical hermeneutics of the "theology of liberation," I enrolled in two New Testament courses: "Revelation" and the "Concept of Person in the New Testament," both were taught by Richard Foulkes. In "Revelation" we studied the literary construction of the book, historical criticism and we discussed its message to the people of Latin America in 1977. To complete the course I wrote a paper on "Reflections on the Roman Empire in Revelation." As an outgrowth of the second course, I wrote a paper on "The Problem of Women in the Writings of Paul."

What is the status of political prisoners and minorities, and what positive actions are being taken to alleviate the conditions of people living under oppressive governments?

From my participation in the Oikoumene Committee and in worship services at Union Seminary, I had become aware of the plight of many people who were resisting fascist regimes in the Third World. The concern for human rights on the part of the World Council of Churches, the United Church Board for World Ministries, as well as the President of the United States, increased my concern. *New optics, compromise, revolution, variant perspectives* and *political options* were relatively new terms in my theological vocabulary before I left for Latin America.

Costa Rica has the reputation of being one of the most stable countries in Latin America. The Constitution of 1949 describes Costa Riça as a "free and independent democratic republic...bounded by the Caribbean Sea, the Pacific Ocean, and the republics of Nicaragua and Panama." Because of its stability, Costa Rica is a refuge for many political prisoners, from both South and Central America.

One priest who had been evicted from El Salvador told us how he had been kidnapped and harrassed for his attempts to form Bible study groups among workers. The Bible is a powerful weapon for it proclaims the good news of liberation to those who are incarcerated, while it threatens others with the Word of justice.

In Nicaragua, after an attack on San Carlos, many Sandinistas escaped over the border to Costa Rica and took up residence in San José. Ernesto Cardenal, priest of the community of Solentiname, Nicaragua, described the fate of his community in an interview with Dow Kirkpatrick on November 9, 1977.

> Some of them had to walk for four days without eating or sleeping in order to arrive at the Costa Rican border. Others were taken prisoners and two more of our community disappeared and nothing more has been heard from them. We don't know whether they are alive. We are afraid that they may be dead because it has been quite some time since that happened. We haven't heard anything of them. Through government reprisal our community has been completely destroyed. They also set fire to some of the *campesinos*' homes. We cannot think of returning to Nicaragua until the fall of President Somoza. We are in exile in Costa Rica.

This report and other similar ones made me realize how intense is the political oppression experienced by both Catholic and Evangelical Nicaraguans who openly confess that "Faith in the New Testament consists in believing that Christ is the Messiah, the Liberator who has come to change the world. And faith consists of change, the Kingdom of a new and just society."

How does "doing theology" in Latin America affect our "doing theology" in the parishes of the United States?

A. Do we "do theology" for Latin Americans in order to help liberate them from their poverty?

B. Do we forget Latin America and concentrate on our own problems because we are realistic enough to realize that we have plenty of them?

C. "With a Bible in one hand and a newspaper in the other" (Karl Barth), do we accept God's call to be the people in the world, being liberated as we liberate others?

Surprisingly, these were some of the first questions that my companions at the seminary asked me. I wasn't long in Costa Rica before I added a new word to my vocabulary--*machismo*. *Machismo* is a feeling of male superiority on the part of a large number of males, and it has come to include a domineering attitude toward women. At the seminary the "*machismo*" mentality is sensed to a lesser degree because of the special efforts of several professors to combat it, including Julia Campos, Richard and Irene Foulkes and Victorio Araya. Julia Campos organized a conference to deal with "Women and a Re-reading of the Bible." We, women and men, were challenged to seek liberation through uniting for complete liberation in Latin America.

Imperialism: I had studied the Babylonian, Roman, Napoleanic and other great empires, but I had no idea that the United States was considered to be an empire. In 1776, we declared our independence from imperialism, while in 1978 we are considered imperialists. The U.S. influences and dominates other cultures often through our products, our movies our TV programs. Who is emperor? Gulf, Kodak and McDonald's are some of the imperial seals that decorate the streets.

FINAL REMARKS

Final conclusion? There is no final conclusion! The experience and friendships of my year in Costa Rica will continue to grow and to gain potency in my life and ministry. After graduation from Union Theological Seminary this summer, I will be ordained to the parish ministry of the United Church of Christ.

The voices of Latin America continue to challenge us. Have we confused our faith with civil religion? Do we go to church several times a week but worship a civil god? Do we abhor violence and murder while we support a system that kills? Do we worship a God of consumerism, one that instantly relieves us of our pain?

Do we worship a God who speaks only English? *Well, God speaks Spanish...and Portuguese!* Most of my friends told me this. I always laughed because, while I had learned in kindergarden that God was red, yellow, black and white, I had never heard that God speaks Spanish and Portuguese. But I believe that it is true. Right before I left the Latin American Biblical Seminary, I agreed. "God does speak Spanish and Portuguese, because now that I can speak Spanish fluently and read Latin American theology in Spanish and Portuguese, I understand more about God."

God is incarnate in the people of Latin America and is speaking through these people to us--in Spanish and Portuguese. Do we listen? Do we allow the grace of God to take over our lives, to lead us in obedience to his will? We continue to be challenged to listen to the Spanish and Portuguese voice of God and to obey. He confronts us in the North. Do time, money and success masquerade as the "Spirit," while the Spirit of the Beatitudes remains in the storage closets with our Bibles?

APPENDIX THREE

THE MINISTRY RECORD

of

The Rev. Dr. Martha Boyer

1971-1975
Student, Carnegie Mellon University
Pittsburgh, Pennsylvania

1975-1978
Student, Union Theological Seminary
New York City, New York

1977
Seminario Bíblico Latineramericano
San José, Costa Rica

1978-1980
Associate Missionary, UCBWM
Fraternal Worker, Evangelische Kirchengemeinde Dietrich Bonhoeffer (Dietrich Bonhoeffer Parish)
West Berlin, Germany

1980
Missionary, UCBWM
Executive Assistant of the Near East Mission
Istanbul, Turkey

1981
Missionary, UCBWM (on medical furlough)
Lancaster, Pennsylvania

1982-1987
Pastor, First United Church of Christ
Warren, Ohio

1987-1988
Interim Minister of Christian Education and Visitation, Trinity United Church of Christ
Wooster, Ohio

1989-1992
Pastor, Pilgrim United Church of Christ
Elyria, Ohio

1992-2001
Pastor, Christ Church, United Church of Christ
Norristown, Pennsylvania

1996-2000
Doctoral Student, Lancaster Theological Seminary
Lancaster, PA

2001-2004
Pastor, St. John's United Church of Christ
Jonestown, Pennsylvania.

2004-2013
Pastor, Solomon's United Church of Christ
Macungie, Pennsylvania

2013-2022
Pastor, St. Paul United Church of Christ
Shrewsbury, Pennsylvania

2023-2024
Supply Pastor, York Association of the UCC
York County, Pennsylvania

NOTES

Chapter One

1. Mitch Leigh and John Darion, "The Impossible Dream (The Quest)," from *Man of La Mancha* (Helena Music Company/Andrew Scott Music, 1965); *passim*.

Chapter Eight

1. Martha Boyer, *Turnabout from the Low Ebb: A Study of How Mid-sized Urban Churches in Transitional Neighborhoods Have Affected Turnabouts in Worship Attendance*, D.Min. diss., Lancaster Theological Seminary (Lancaster, PA), 2000.

Chapter Nine

1. Leo Newhouse, "Is Crying Good for You?" *Harvard Health Blog* (March 1, 2021), online.

2. Nancy Sokarno, quoted by Maggie Zhou, in "Sad Girl TV: Why Consuming Depressing Content Hurts So Good," *Refinery29* (May 5, 2022), online.

3. I considered labeling this section "Take Time for Silliness." After a Bible study on the word "silly," I find it to be a pejorative and a synonym for fool. Silliness is sometimes described negatively as in this passage in which Paul states: "You foolish Galatians! Who has bewitched you? It was before your eyes that Jesus Christ was publicly exhibited as crucified!"(Galatians 3:1) Following Christ demands a certain amount of seriousness and solemnity, but one cannot reach true sense of Shalom without

developing an authentic sense of humor, even a little silliness.

Chapter Eleven

1. "Sing" by Lea Salonga (1972).

2. "Let There Be Peace on Earth" by Jill Jackson-Miller and Sy Miller (1983).

3. United States Library of Congress, "Collection: The Library of Congress Celebrates the Songs of America," online exhibition, https://www.loc.gov/collections/songs-of-america/articles-and-essays/musical-styles/ritual-and-worship/spirituals/.

4. Aaron Cooley, "War on Poverty," *Britannica* (May 30, 2014), online, https://www.britannica.com/topic/War-on-Poverty.

5. Jewish Community Center (York, PA),

6. I have recently discovered the National Alliance on Mental Illness (NAMI) online. Founded in 1979, NAMI is the nation's largest grassroots organization for mental illness awareness and support. Online, visit them at https://www.nami.org/.

Chapter Twelve

1. "What Does it Mean That There is a Time to Embrace and a Time to Refrain from Embracing (Ecclesiastes 3:5)?" *Got Questions* (n.d), online, https://www.gotquestions.org/time-to-embrace-and-time-to-refrain-embracing.html.

2. Francis McGlone and Susannah Walker, "Four Ways Hugs Are Good for Your Health," *Greater Good Magazine* (June 22,

2021), online, https://greatergood.berkeley.edu/article/item/four_ways_hugs_are_good_for_your_health.

Chapter Thirteen

1. Bertolt Brecht, "A Worker Reads History," AllPoetry, online, https://allpoetry.com/A-Worker-Reads-History.

2. Dietrich Bonhoeffer, "Who Am I?", DBonhoeffer.org, online, http://www.dbonhoeffer.org/who-was-db2.htm.

Chapter Fourteen

1. See Ken Duckworth, *You Are Not Alone: the NAMI Guide for Navigating Mental Health* (Zando, 2022).

Chapter Fifteen

1. Henri Nouwen, *The Wounded Healer* (Image, 1979), 4.

Chapter Sixteen

1. Cleveland Clinic, "Dopamine," The Cleveland Clinic (March 23, 2022), online, https://my.clevelandclinic.org/health/articles/22581-dopamine.

2. Elisabeth Kübler-Ross, *On Death & Dying* (Scribner, 1969).

Chapter Eighteen

1. United Church of Christ, "Statement of Faith of the United Church of Christ—La Declaración de Fe de la Iglesia Unida de Cristo," United Church o Christ, online, https://www.ucc.org/what-we-believe/worship/statement-of-faith/.

Appendix Two

1. Martha Helene Butkofsky, "A Theological-Educational Experience in Latin America," published in the missilogical journal of CELEP (The Latin American Center for Evangelical Studies), published in San José, California, by Orlado Costas (February, 1978).

Barber's Son Press
York, Pennsylvania

www.ingramcontent.com/pod-product-compliance
Lightning Source LLC
Chambersburg PA
CBHW050809160426
43192CB00010B/1694